D0118293

100 HEALTHY RECIPES

Healing Vegetarian Recipes

DELICIOUS RECIPES FOR BODY AND MIND

100 HEALTHY RECIPES

Healing Vegetarian Recipes

DELICIOUS RECIPES FOR BODY AND MIND

hamlyn

Healing Vegetarian Recipes

First published in 2017 by Bounty Books,
a division of Octopus Publishing Group Ltd
Carmelite House
50 Victoria Embankment
London, EC4Y 0DZ
www.octopusbooks.co.uk

Published in 2018 by Bounty Books for Hamlyn,
a division of Octopus Publishing Group Ltd

Copyright © Octopus Publishing Group Ltd 2017,
2018

All rights reserved. No part of this work may
be reproduced or utilised in any form or by
any means, electronic or mechanical, including
photcopying, recording, or by any information
storage and retrieval system, without the prior
written permission of the publishers.

ISBN: 978-0-753732-88-5

A CIP catalogue record for this book is available
from the British Library

Printed and bound in China

10 9 8 7 6 5 4 3 2 1

Publisher: Lucy Pessell
Editor: Sarah Vaughan
Project Editor: Jane Birch
Designer: Lisa Layton
Design: Chris Bell/cbdesign
Production Controller: Beata Kibil

Contents

introduction

There are lots of reasons to choose a vegetarian diet: many people are vegetarian on religious or ethical grounds, it is more sustainable for the planet to grow food to feed ourselves rather than animals, and a vegetarian diet is wallet-friendly too. A diet based on meat is calculated to be about twice as expensive as a vegetarian one. But a really excellent reason for being vegetarian is the benefit to your health.

A diet rich in fresh vegetables, fruit, legumes and wholegrains is well documented to be a healthy one and, with such an abundance of wonderful seasonal vegetables widely available, it's not hard to see why many people choose to become vegetarian or opt to add more meat-free meals to the menu.

Research has shown that cutting meat usually means getting more dietary fiber, folic acid, vitamins C and E, potassium, magnesium and unsaturated fat, and less unhealthy saturated fat and cholesterol.

From smoothies and salads to soups and stir-fries, the delicious recipes in this collection are targeted at different aspects of health and wellbeing. So, whether you want something for a specific ailment or all-round health booster, you'll be able to find the healing recipe you need.

ENSURING A BALANCED DIET

A properly balanced vegetarian diet will supply all the nutrients your body requires for optimum health and makes it easier for you to get your all-important "five a day" of fruit and vegetables.

The key to a well-balanced diet is simple: eat plenty of wholegrains and legumes, vegetables and fruit. It's important to include protein in your daily diet, although we do not need large amounts of it. Good vegetarian sources are legumes such as chickpeas, lentils, milk, cheese, yogurt, soya products, oats and nuts and seeds.

Dairy products, such as butter, cheese, cream, milk and yogurt, or non-dairy alternatives should form a smaller part of your diet. Alcohol and sugary treats should be enjoyed in moderation.

VITAMINS AND MINERALS

Vegetarians need to pay attention to some specific vitamins and minerals and be sure to include them, as deficiencies can affect health and vitality. These are:

Calcium Many dairy products contain calcium; it is also available by eating nuts, seeds and beans.

Iron There are two types of iron: haeme iron, from meat, poultry and fish, and non-haeme iron, from vegetables and dairy products. Although haeme iron is more easily absorbed than vegetarian non-haeme iron, good sources of non-haeme iron include tofu, soy beans and green vegetables such as spinach, lentils and beans. Combining iron-rich foods with ingredients that contain vitamin C in your meals will help iron absorption.

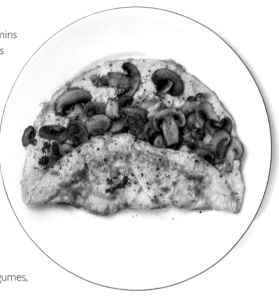

Zinc Veggie-friendly foods that can provide zinc are legumes, eggs, nuts and seeds.

Riboflavin (Vitamin B2) Among other things, riboflavin is responsible for maintaining healthy eyes, skin and nervous system. Sources of riboflavin include eggs, most cereals, mushrooms and milk.

Vitamin B12 You only need to find a few micrograms on a daily basis in order to get sufficient vitamin B12. You can find this in eggs, soy milk, cheese, yeast extract and yogurt.

VARIETY IS THE SPICE OF LIFE

As children we might have been told to "eat our greens", but now health experts agree it's just as important to eat our reds, oranges, yellows, blues and purples too. Aim to eat a range of vegetables of various colors each day and add variety to your plate by trying different vegetable combinations for pastas, salads, stews and stir-fries.

READ THE LABEL

Not all products are suitable for vegetarians, so it's best to check the packaging. For example, some sweets contain gelatine, animal rennet is often used in cheese-making and some curry pastes contain shrimp. Mostly, there are vegetarian alternatives that you can select instead.

STORE CUPBOARD STAPLES

Pasta & noodles It's helpful to have a variety of dried pasta shapes – such as linguini or spaghetti, fusilli and penne – to hand. You'll also find a huge selection of noodles available at the supermarket. Choose one or two from soba, udon, bean thread, ramen, vermicelli and flat rice noodles.

Rice Keep a selection of basmati, brown, risotto and jasmine rice.

Legumes & beans You'll need a variety of these, including red kidney beans, butter beans, cannellini beans, dried red lentils, green and Puy lentils and chickpeas.

Wholegrains There are a few to consider to trying: quinoa, which actually a seed, is high in protein, quick to cook and has a chewy, slightly nutty flavor. Even higher in protein and fiber is freekeh which is wheat that's harvested while young and green. It's roasted over an open fire, then the straw and chaff are burned and rubbed off, leaving a slightly chewy grain with a distinctive taste. Other options are barley, millet and buckwheat.

Nuts & seeds Wholesome and delicious, these perk up many dishes, including salads and stir-fries. Good ones to have in stock are pine nuts, cashew nuts, walnuts, sunflower seeds, pumpkin seeds, chia seeds and linseed.

Cans Packed with flavor, canned chopped, plum and cherry tomatoes and passata are a terrific standby for adding to sauces, curries, soups and stews. Coconut milk is also great to have to hand for Asian-style curries and soups.

Oils Olive oil is essential and you should also have extra-virgin olive oil for salad dressings. Sunflower, groundnut and sesame oils are useful too.

Vegetable stock You can make your own (see opposite for a recipe) or use good-quality stock cubes or bouillon powder. Some stock cubes or powders can be very salty, so look for the salt-reduced versions.

Spices A well-stocked kitchen has a selection of these, including ground cilantro, cumin, paprika, cinnamon, ginger, nutmeg, turmeric, mustard seeds and chili flakes. More unusual Moroccan spice blends like ras-el-hanout and za'atar are great too.

Condiments Soy sauce is excellent for adding a salty hit to vegetarian Thai dishes, in place of fish sauce. Other key condiments to keep in your cupboard are tomato ketchup, wasabi paste, sweet chilli sauce and one or two types of mustard – wholegrain, Dijon and English, for instance.

Vinegars Red wine, white wine, balsamic, cider and rice vinegars are all a must for creating salad dressings and sauces.

Pastes Fiery harissa used as condiment or ingredient gives a real flavor boost and ready-made curry pastes, such as tikka and korma, are great for creating a speedy meal. Be careful when choosing Thai-style pastes, as many of these may contain shrimp. Chipotle paste adds a smoky chilli flavor to Mexican-inspired dishes. Tahini is essential if you are planning on making hummus and can also be added to salad dressings and sauces.

IN THE FRIDGE

Tofu Also called bean curd, tofu is made from soy beans. It's extremely versatile and can be used in stir-fries, casseroles and soups.

Cheese This is a source of protein for vegetarians but always check the label as some hard cheeses are made with animal rennet.

Dairy products Staples are milk, butter and natural yogurt. Crème fraîche is useful too. You can also use non-dairy versions of these, if you prefer.

Fresh fruit & veg Salad leaves, limes, lemons and scallions are all key ingredients to keep in supply.

IN THE PANTRY

Garlic, onions, potatoes, shallots, carrots and other root vegetables and most varieties of fruit will keep well for a few days in the pantry. Aim to buy fruit and vegetables in season and, ideally, locally grown. Buy the best quality you can afford, to deliver maximum health benefits.

ON THE WINDOWSILL

Nothing takes a dish from good to great like fresh herbs. Pots of easy-to-grow basil, mint, cilantro and parsley will add color to your kitchen windowsill and give loads of flavor to recipes.

VEGETABLE STOCK

1 tablespoon olive oil
5 carrots, finely chopped
2 celery sticks with leaves, finely chopped
2 onions, finely chopped
2 leeks, finely sliced
1 fennel bulb, chopped
1 garlic bulb, unpeeled and roughly chopped
1 thyme sprig
1 rosemary sprig
1 bay leaf
handful of parsley
small bunch of basil
4 litres (7 pints) water
1 teaspoon sea salt
1 teaspoon black peppercorns

MAKES 4 litres (7 pints)

Heat the oil in a large stockpot and sweat all the vegetables and the garlic for 5–6 minutes.

Add the herbs, water, sea salt and peppercorns and bring to the boil, then lower the heat and simmer for 1½–2 hours, skimming occasionally.

Strain the stock through a sieve and let it cool.

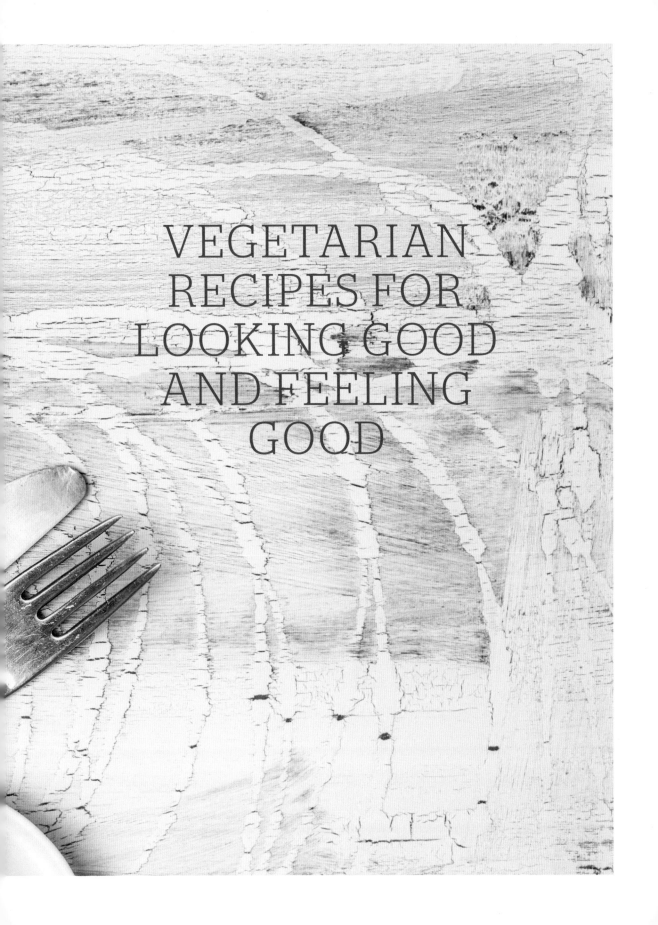

VEGETARIAN RECIPES FOR LOOKING GOOD AND FEELING GOOD

introduction

To look and feel good, you have to give your body what it needs to thrive. A diet that contains too much fat, sugar and processed foods will take its toll but, if you opt for a wholesome diet full of vitamins and minerals, your body reflects it - you feel fit and energized.

Eating right will give your body every benefit, from radiant skin to stronger muscles. And for eating right, a nutrient-rich vegetarian diet, packed with veggies and fruit, is an excellent choice. Research shows that the greater the proportion of vegetables and fruit in your diet, the lower the risk of heart disease, diabetes and cancer too.

From a skin-enhancing curry to a detox smoothie and from a brain-building salad to an immune-boosting soup, the recipes in this chapter are aimed at providing the nourishment needed for looking and feeling your best, from head to toe.

ENERGY

arugula & goats' cheese omelette

THE SCIENCE BIT

Our bodies needs fuel to function well so try to eat regularly to keep your energy and mood levels stable.

SERVES 4
Prep + cook time: 20 minutes

12 eggs
4 tablespoons milk
4 tablespoons chopped mixed herbs,
  such as chervil, chives, marjoram,
  parsley and tarragon
50 g (2 oz) butter
125 g (4 oz) soft goats' cheese,
  diced
small handful of baby arugula leaves
salt and pepper

Beat the eggs, milk, herbs and salt and pepper together in a large bowl. Melt a quarter of the butter in an omelette pan. As soon as it stops foaming, swirl in a quarter of the egg mixture and cook over a medium heat, forking over the omelette so that it cooks evenly.

As soon as it is set on the underside but still a little runny in the center, scatter a quarter of the cheese and a quarter of the arugula leaves over one half of the omelette.

Carefully slide the omelette onto a serving plate, folding it in half as you go. For the best results, serve immediately, then repeat to make 3 more omelettes and serve each individually. Alternatively, keep warm in a moderate oven and serve all at the same time.

Omelettes make a great lunch or breakfast choice as the protein in eggs provides sustained energy for a busy day.

ENERGY

oven-baked squash with quinoa

THE SCIENCE BIT

Gluten-free and packed with protein, quinoa is also a nutrient-dense source of carbohydrates for long-lasting energy.

SERVES 4

Prep + cook time: 50 minutes

2 tablespoons olive oil
750 g (1½ lb) butternut squash, peeled, deseeded and cut into 3.5 cm (1½ inch) chunks
25 g (1 oz) butter
1 red onion, chopped
1 garlic clove, crushed
50 g (2 oz) pine nuts
300 g (10 oz) quinoa
150 ml (¼ pint) dry white wine
1 cinnamon stick
1 litre (1¾ pints) vegetable stock (see page 9 for homemade)
4 tablespoons chopped mint
200 g (7 oz) feta cheese, crumbled
100 g (3½ oz) pomegranate seeds
salt and pepper

Heat the oil in a large frying pan and add the squash in a single layer. Season well with salt and pepper and cook over a medium heat for about 10 minutes until lightly browned.

Meanwhile, melt the butter in a flameproof casserole dish, add the onion and garlic and cook for 2–3 minutes until softened. Stir in the pine nuts and quinoa and cook for 1 minute or until the quinoa is starting to pop. Add the wine and cook until it has been absorbed.

Stir in the squash, cinnamon stick and stock. Bring to the boil, season to taste with salt and pepper and stir well.

Cover the dish with the lid and cook in a preheated oven, 190°C (375°F) for 25 minutes until the quinoa is just tender.

Stir in the mint, then scatter over the feta and pomegranate seeds. Serve immediately.

ENERGY

bean, lemon & rosemary hummus

THE SCIENCE BIT

The low-GI butter beans in this hummus are digested slowly to provide sustained energy and are also a good source of vegetarian protein.

SERVES 4–6

Prep + cook time: 20 minutes
  + cooling

6 tablespoons extra-virgin olive oil,
   plus extra to serve
4 shallots, finely chopped
2 large garlic cloves, crushed
1 teaspoon chopped rosemary, plus
   extra sprigs to garnish
grated rind and juice of ½ lemon
2 x 400 g (13 oz) cans butter beans,
   rinsed and drained
salt and pepper
toasted ciabatta, to serve

Heat the oil in a frying pan, add the shallots, garlic, chopped rosemary and lemon rind and cook over a low heat, stirring occasionally, for 10 minutes until the shallots are softened. Leave to cool.

Transfer the shallot mixture to a food processor or blender, add all the remaining ingredients and process until smooth.

Spread the hummus on to toasted ciabatta, garnish with rosemary sprigs and serve drizzled with oil.

Garlic is best stored at room temperature in a cool, dark place away from exposure to heat and sunlight to help prevent sprouting.

ENERGY

minestrone with pasta & beans

THE SCIENCE BIT

All B vitamins help in converting food into energy so getting your recommended daily requirement ensures your body has a reliable source of energy to call on.

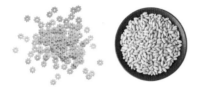

SERVES 4

Prep + cook time: 40 minutes

2 tablespoons olive oil

1 onion, chopped

1 celery stick, chopped

1 carrot, chopped

1 garlic clove, crushed

400 g (13 oz) can chopped tomatoes

1.5 litres (2½ pints) vegetable stock (see page 9 for homemade)

1 rosemary sprig

150 g (5 oz) small soup pasta

75 g (3 oz) cavolo nero or other cabbage, shredded

200 g (7 oz) canned cannellini beans, rinsed and drained

4 tablespoons fresh green pesto

25 g (1 oz) Parmesan-style cheese, grated

salt and pepper

crusty bread, to serve

Heat the oil in a large, heavy-based saucepan. Add the onion, celery and carrot and cook for 5 minutes until softened, then add the garlic and cook for a further 1 minute. Pour in the tomatoes and stock, add the rosemary and bring to the boil. Reduce the heat and simmer for 15 minutes.

Add the pasta and cabbage and cook for 5–7 minutes, or according to packet instructions. Stir in the beans and heat through, then season to taste.

Ladle the soup into bowls, drizzle with the pesto, and sprinkle with the cheese. Serve with chunks of crusty bread.

For homemade pesto place 75 g (3 oz) basil leaves, 50 g (2 oz) pine nuts and 2 garlic cloves in a food processor and process until well blended. Then stir in 50 g (2 oz) grated vegetarian Parmesan-style cheese and 100 ml (3½ fl oz) olive oil.

Japanese-style guacamole

THE SCIENCE BIT

Avocado can do wonders for your skin – the oils in it keep skin supple and it has vitamin E to support healthy skin growth.

SERVES 4
Prep time: 15 minutes

2 ripe avocados
juice of 2 small limes
1–2 teaspoons wasabi paste, to taste
4 scallions, finely chopped
1 tablespoon sesame seeds, toasted
1 teaspoon mirin
1 teaspoon finely chopped pickled
  ginger
sesame seeds, for sprinkling
prawn or rice crackers, to serve

Cut the avocados in half and remove and discard the pits. Peel off the skin and roughly chop the flesh. Place in a bowl and roughly mash with a fork.

Stir in the lime juice, wasabi, scallions, sesame seeds and mirin.

Transfer to a serving bowl and scatter over the pickled ginger and sesame seeds. Serve immediately, with crackers for dipping.

Fiery wasabi is one of the main flavorings of Japanese food. It's quite pungent, so be careful not to use too much as it will overwhelm the other ingredients in this guacamole.

SKIN

pomegranate & granola smoothie

THE SCIENCE BIT

A 2007 study found that people who regularly ate vitamin C-rich foods, like pomegranate and mango, had fewer wrinkles and less age-related dry skin.

SERVES 4

Prep time: 10 minutes

750 ml (1¼ pint) pomegranate juice
2 tablespoons pomegranate molasses
500 g (1 lb) fresh or frozen mango pieces
125 g (4 oz) granola
1–2 tablespoons agave nectar or runny honey
4 scoops frozen natural yogurt
100 g (3½ oz) pomegranate seeds (optional)

Place all the ingredients except the frozen yogurt and pomegranate seeds, if using, in a blender or food processor and blend until smooth. This may need to be done in 2 batches.

Take 4 glasses and place 1 scoop of frozen yogurt in each. Pour the smoothie over the yogurt, sprinkle over pomegranate seeds, if using, and serve immediately.

Made from the sap of various species of the succulent, agave, agave nectar is available in light and dark varieties and can be used as an alternative to honey or sugar.

SKIN

red beet chilli & papaya salsa

THE SCIENCE BIT

The kidney beans in this salsa contain zinc to help heal blemishes, while tomatoes and red beets are full of vitamin C for a radiant complexion.

SERVES 4

Prep + cook time: 2 hours

1 tablespoon sunflower oil

1 onion, chopped

2 garlic cloves, finely chopped

500 g (1 lb) raw red beets, peeled and cubed

400 g (13 oz) can red kidney beans, rinsed and drained

1–2 teaspoons dried chili flakes, to taste

2 teaspoons paprika

1 teaspoon ground cinnamon

400 g (13 oz) can chopped tomatoes

450 ml (¾ pint) vegetable stock (see page 9 for homemade)

2 tablespoons red wine vinegar

1 tablespoon brown sugar

1 papaya, peeled, deseeded and diced

½ small red onion, finely chopped

1 tomato, deseeded and diced

small bunch of cilantro, roughly chopped

salt and pepper

Heat the oil in a flameproof casserole, add the onion and fry for 5 minutes until lightly browned. Mix in the garlic, red beets, kidney beans, chili flakes and spices, then add the tomatoes, stock, vinegar, sugar and plenty of seasoning.

Bring to the boil then cover and cook in a preheated oven, 180°C (350°F) for 1½ hours or until the red beets is tender.

Meanwhile, make the salsa. Mix together the papaya, red onion, tomato and cilantro and spoon into a serving dish.

Spoon the chilli into bowls and top with spoonfuls of the salsa. Serve with brown rice or warmed tortillas and a dollop of soured cream, if liked.

Thai massaman pumpkin curry

THE SCIENCE BIT

Carotenoids in the bright orange flesh of pumpkin defend skin cells from oxidative damage and pumpkin also provides skin-protecting vitamin C.

SERVES 4

Prep + cook time: 30 minutes

2 tablespoons vegetable oil

2 tablespoons Thai massaman curry
    paste

6 shallots, thinly sliced

8 cm (3 inch) length of trimmed
    lemongrass stalk, finely chopped

6 green cardamom pods

2 teaspoons black mustard seeds

800 g (1¾ lb) pumpkin flesh, cut
    into 1 cm (½ inch) cubes

200 ml (7 fl oz) hot vegetable stock
    (see page 9 for homemade)

400 ml (14 fl oz) can coconut milk

juice of 1 lime

Thai basil or mint leaves and red
    chilli slivers, to garnish

lime wedges and steamed jasmine
    rice, to serve (optional)

Heat the oil in a heavy-based saucepan, add the curry paste, shallots, lemongrass, cardamom and mustard seeds and fry over a medium heat for 1–2 minutes until fragrant.

Add the pumpkin and pour over the stock and coconut milk. Bring to a simmer, then cook for 10–12 minutes or until the pumpkin is tender.

Remove from the heat and stir in the lime juice. Ladle into bowls, scatter with Thai basil or mint leaves and red chilli slivers and serve with lime wedges for squeezing over and steamed jasmine rice, if liked.

One of the most important ways to take care of your skin and avoid wrinkles, age spots and an increased risk of skin cancer is to protect it from the sun, so don't forget the SPF.

sage & tomato pilaf

THE SCIENCE BIT

Tomatoes contain carotenoids, the compounds that give them their red color, which are thought to help decrease the risk of many eye diseases.

SERVES 4

Prep + cook time: 55 minutes

500 g (1 lb) plum tomatoes
1 red pepper, cored, deseeded and
   quartered
1 onion, roughly chopped
2 tablespoons olive oil
small bunch of sage
200 g (7 oz) easy-cook long-grain
   white and wild rice mixed
salt and pepper

Cut each tomato into 8 and thickly slice the pepper quarters. Place in a roasting tin with the onion, then drizzle with the oil and season well. Tear some of the sage into pieces and sprinkle over the vegetables. Roast in a preheated oven, 200°C (400°F) for 40–45 minutes until softened.

Meanwhile, cook the rice in a saucepan of boiling water for 15 minutes until only just cooked. Drain, rinse in cold water and drain again well. Mix the rice into the cooked tomatoes and peppers.

Stir well then spoon into bowls and sprinkle with the remaining sage leaves.

As well as upping overall health, exercise is good for your eyes. Some studies suggest that regular exercise, such as walking, can reduce the risk of age-related macular degeneration by as much as 70 per cent.

fennel, pernod & orange casserole

THE SCIENCE BIT

Fennel and tomatoes are both brimming with vitamin C which numerous studies have linked with a decreased risk of cataracts.

SERVES 4

Prep + cook time: about 1 hour

2 fennel bulbs, trimmed
4 tablespoons extra-virgin olive oil
1 onion, chopped
2 garlic cloves, crushed
2 teaspoons chopped rosemary
100 ml (3½ fl oz) Pernod
400 g (13 oz) can chopped
  tomatoes
¼ teaspoon saffron threads
2 strips of orange rind
2 tablespoons chopped fennel
  fronds
salt and pepper

Cut the fennel lengthways into 5 mm (¼ inch) thick slices. Heat half the oil in a flameproof casserole, add the fennel slices, in batches, and cook over a medium heat for 3–4 minutes on each side until golden. Remove with a slotted spoon.

Heat the remaining oil in the casserole, add the onion, garlic, rosemary and salt and pepper and cook over a low heat, stirring frequently, for 5 minutes. Add the Pernod, bring to the boil and boil until reduced by half. Add the tomatoes, saffron and orange rind and stir well. Arrange the fennel slices over the top.

Bring the casserole to the boil, then cover with a tight-fitting lid and bake in a preheated oven, 180°C (350°F) for 35 minutes until the fennel is tender. Stir in the fennel fronds and serve the casserole immediately.

lemongrass & sweet potato curry

THE SCIENCE BIT

Spinach makes this curry particularly eye-friendly as it is full of lutein and zeaxanthin, pigments that can help to prevent macular degeneration.

SERVES 4

Prep + cook time: 35 minutes

2 lemongrass stalks

400 ml (13 fl oz) can coconut milk

150 ml (¼ pint) vegetable stock (see page 9 for homemade)

1 garlic clove, crushed

2.5 cm (1 inch) piece of fresh ginger, peeled and finely chopped

1 red chilli, deseeded and chopped

2 teaspoons palm sugar or soft light brown sugar

6 kaffir lime leaves

450 g (14½ oz) sweet potatoes, peeled and chopped

1 red pepper, cored, deseeded and chopped

200 g (7 oz) baby spinach leaves

2 tablespoons lime juice

handful of cilantro or Thai basil leaves

steamed jasmine rice, to serve

Remove the tough outer stems from the lemongrass, then cut into 2.5 cm (1 inch) pieces.

Place the coconut milk, stock, garlic, ginger, chilli, lemon grass, sugar and lime leaves in a large saucepan and bring to the boil. Add the sweet potatoes, cover and simmer for 10 minutes.

Add the red pepper to the pan and cook for a further 5 minutes.

Stir in the spinach and lime juice, re-cover and cook for 2–3 minutes until the spinach has wilted, then stir in the cilantro or Thai basil. Serve immediately with steamed jasmine rice.

Hugely versatile sweet potatoes – you can enjoy them baked, mashed, roasted and in salads – contain iron, potassium, magnesium, vitamin C and vitamin D.

roasted cauliflower & cashew salad

THE SCIENCE BIT

The cashew nuts in this tasty warm salad are rich in omega-3 fatty acids and vitamin E to boost eye health.

SERVES 4

Prep + cook time: 30 minutes

1 large cauliflower, cut into florets
400 g (13 oz) can chickpeas, rinsed and drained
1 teaspoon cumin seeds
1 teaspoon cilantro seeds
½ teaspoon ground turmeric
½ teaspoon ground ginger
½ teaspoon garam masala
4 tablespoons olive oil
100 g (3½ oz) cashew nuts
150 g (5 oz) natural yogurt
4 tablespoons lemon juice
½ teaspoon Dijon mustard
150 g (5 oz) baby spinach leaves
salt and pepper

Place the cauliflower in a roasting tin with the chickpeas, spices, some salt and pepper and 2 tablespoons of the oil. Roast in a preheated oven, 220°C (425°F) for 15 minutes, then toss in the cashew nuts and roast for a further 10 minutes.

Meanwhile, whisk together the remaining oil, yogurt, lemon juice and mustard to make a dressing.

Put the spinach on a large serving plate and spoon over the spiced cauliflower. Drizzle with the yogurt dressing and serve.

Protect your vision by eating cauliflower – it's high in vitamin C to reduce the risk of age-related macular degeneration.

spicy lentil & carrot soup

THE SCIENCE BIT

Choose lentils for lustrous hair as iron is crucial for feeding the hair follicles and roots and too little iron in the diet can lead to hair loss.

SERVES 4

Prep + cook time: 40 minutes

2 tablespoons sunflower oil
1 garlic clove, finely chopped
1 teaspoon peeled and grated fresh ginger
1 red chilli, finely chopped
1 onion, finely chopped
1 tablespoon sweet smoked paprika
700 g (1½ lb) carrots, finely chopped
150 g (5 oz) red split lentils, rinsed and drained
150 ml (¼ pint) single cream
1 litre (1¾ pints) hot vegetable stock (see page 9 for homemade)
100 ml (3½ fl oz) crème fraîche
small handful of chopped cilantro leaves
salt and pepper

caramelized onions
1 tablespoon butter
1 tablespoon olive oil
1 onion, thinly sliced

Heat the sunflower oil in a heavy-based saucepan, add the garlic, ginger, red chilli, onion and smoked paprika and cook, stirring, over a medium-high heat for 1–2 minutes. Add the carrots, lentils, cream and stock and bring to the boil, then reduce the heat to medium and simmer, uncovered, for 15–20 minutes.

Meanwhile, to make the caramelized onions, heat the butter and olive oil in a frying pan, add the onion and cook over a low heat for 12–15 minutes or until caramelized and golden brown. Drain on kitchen paper and keep warm.

Blend until smooth and then season well.

Ladle into bowls, add a dollop of crème fraiche and scatter with chopped cilantro leaves and the caramelized onions. Sprinkle with a little smoked paprika before serving, if liked.

roasted sweet potato salad

THE SCIENCE BIT

Beta-carotene in sweet potato is converted in the body to vitamin A, essential for hair growth. Vitamin A deficiency can cause dull, damaged hair.

SERVES 4

Prep + cook time: 50 minutes + cooling

500 g (1 lb) sweet potatoes, peeled and cubed
2 tablespoons extra-virgin olive oil
1 teaspoon ground cilantro
½ teaspoon ground cumin
¼ teaspoon ground cinnamon
175 g (6 oz) green beans
150 g (5 oz) baby spinach leaves
50 g (2 oz) shelled pistachio nuts, toasted
salt and pepper

dressing
2 tablespoons natural yogurt
1 small garlic clove, crushed
1 large red chilli, deseeded and finely chopped
1 tablespoon lemon juice
1 teaspoon clear honey
50 ml (2 fl oz) extra-virgin olive oil

Put the sweet potatoes in a roasting tin. Combine the oil, spices and salt and pepper to taste in a small bowl, pour over the potatoes and stir well to evenly coat.

Roast in a preheated oven, 220°C (425°F) for 30–35 minutes, stirring halfway through, until golden and tender. Leave to cool for 30 minutes.

Meanwhile, blanch the beans in a saucepan of lightly salted boiling water for 2–3 minutes until just tender. Drain and refresh under cold water. Drain again and pat dry.

Put the beans in a large bowl with the cooled sweet potatoes, spinach leaves and pistachio nuts.

Make the dressing. Mix together the yogurt, garlic, chilli, lemon juice, honey and salt and pepper to taste in a bowl. Whisk in the oil until evenly blended. Pour over the salad, stir well and serve.

HAIR

honey roast figs

THE SCIENCE BIT

Nutrients including magnesium and vitamins A, C and E stimulate blood circulation in the scalp, accelerating hair growth.

SERVES 2
Prep + cook time: 25 minutes

6 ripe fresh figs
1 tablespoon clear honey
grated rind and juice 1 orange
pinch of ground cinnamon
2 tablespoons crème fraîche
1 tablespoon chopped mint

Cut a deep cross in each fig and place them in an ovenproof dish.

Mix together the honey, orange rind and juice and cinnamon and pour over the figs. Cook in a preheated oven, 190°C (375°F) for about 20 minutes or until bubbling and the figs are soft.

Mix together the crème fraîche and mint and serve with the figs.

Used frequently in Chinese herbal medicine, fragrant cinnamon contains antioxidants to help protect the body from disease.

minted pea & sesame falafel

THE SCIENCE BIT

Strong, shiny hair needs protein which the ingredients in this recipe – peas, chickpeas, sesame seeds and yogurt – provide in abundance.

SERVES 4
Prep + cook time: 30 minutes

250 g (8 oz) frozen peas, just
  defrosted
2 x 400 g (13 oz) cans chickpeas,
  rinsed and drained
1 onion, quartered
1½ teaspoons cumin seeds, crushed
1½ teaspoons cilantro seeds,
  crushed
1 teaspoon ground turmeric
3 tablespoons chopped mint
2 tablespoons sesame seeds
1 tablespoon plain flour
3 tablespoons olive oil
salt and pepper

radish cacik
200 g (7 oz) natural yogurt
100 g (3½ oz) radishes, finely diced
5 cm (2 inch) piece of cucumber,
  finely diced
2 tablespoons chopped mint

Finely chop the peas, chickpeas and onion together in a blender or food processor. Alternatively, chop them finely with a knife. Mix in the crushed seeds, turmeric, mint and seasoning.

Spoon 20 mounds of the mixture on to a baking sheet, then roll into ovals with the palms of your hands. Mix the sesame seeds and flour on a plate, then roll the falafel in the mixture and return to the baking sheet.

Mix all the cacik ingredients together, season to taste and spoon into a serving bowl.

Heat 2 tablespoons of the oil in a large frying pan, add the falafel and fry, turning, until golden brown and piping hot, adding the remaining oil if needed.

Serve immediately with the cacik.

BRAIN

quinoa porridge with raspberries

THE SCIENCE BIT

Vitamin E, found in seeds, is thought to help prevent cognitive decline and pumpkin seeds are especially full of zinc, vital for enhancing memory and thinking skills.

SERVES 2
Prep + cook time: 35 minutes

600 ml (1 pint) milk
100 g (3½ oz) quinoa
2 tablespoons superfine sugar
½ teaspoon ground cinnamon
125 g (4 oz) fresh raspberries
2 tablespoons mixed seeds, such
   as sunflower, linseed, pumpkin
   and hemp
2 tablespoons clear honey

Bring the milk to the boil in a small saucepan. Add the quinoa and return to the boil. Reduce the heat to low, cover and simmer for about 15 minutes until three-quarters of the milk has been absorbed.

Stir the sugar and cinnamon into the pan, re-cover and cook for 8–10 minutes or until almost all the milk has been absorbed and the quinoa is tender.

Spoon the porridge into 2 bowls, then top with the raspberries, sprinkle over the seeds and drizzle with the honey. Serve immediately.

Start a busy day with this porridge. Low-GI quinoa releases glucose slowly into the blood stream, keeping you mentally alert all day.

pancakes with blueberry sauce

THE SCIENCE BIT

Researchers believe that the antioxidants in blueberries stimulate the flow of blood and oxygen to the brain and keep the memory fresh.

SERVES 4–6

Prep + cook time: 30 minutes

15 g (½ oz) butter
150 g (5 oz) self-raising flour
1 teaspoon bicarbonate of soda
40 g (1½ oz) superfine sugar
1 egg, beaten
350 ml (12 fl oz) buttermilk
icing sugar, for dusting (optional)
Greek yogurt or crème fraîche,
  to serve

blueberry sauce
250 g (8 oz) fresh blueberries
2 tablespoons clear honey
dash of lemon juice

Heat the blueberries with the honey and lemon juice in a small saucepan over a low heat for about 3 minutes until they release their juices. Keep warm.

Melt the butter in a separate small saucepan. Sift the flour and bicarbonate of soda into a bowl and stir in the superfine sugar. Beat the egg and buttermilk together in a separate bowl or jug, then gradually whisk into the dry ingredients with the melted butter to make a smooth batter.

Heat a nonstick frying pan until hot. Drop in large spoonfuls of the batter and cook over a high heat for 3 minutes until bubbles appear on the surface. Flip the pancakes over and cook for a further minute. Remove and keep warm in a moderate oven. Repeat with the remaining batter.

Serve the pancakes topped with the blueberry sauce and Greek-style yogurt or crème fraîche, and dusted with icing sugar, if liked.

red beets risotto with goats' cheese

THE SCIENCE BIT

Boost your brainpower with red beets. It contains natural nitrates to increase blood flow to the brain for better mental performance.

SERVES 4

Prep + cook time: 40 minutes

1 tablespoon vegetable oil
1 onion, finely chopped
1 garlic clove, finely chopped
250 g (8 oz) risotto rice
100 ml (3½ fl oz) dry white wine
900 ml (1½ pints) hot vegetable
   stock (see page 9 for homemade)
500 g (1 lb) cooked red beets
   (not in vinegar), diced
25 g (1 oz) butter
100 g (3½ oz) goats' cheese
salt and pepper
handful of chopped dill, to garnish

Heat the oil in a large, heavy-based saucepan. Add the onion and cook for 5 minutes until softened. Add the garlic and rice and cook for 30 seconds until coated in the oil. Pour in the wine and bubble until boiled away.

Gradually add the stock, a ladleful at a time, stirring continuously and allowing each ladleful to be absorbed before adding the next. This should take about 15 minutes.

Meanwhile, place half the red beets in a food processor or blender with a little of the stock and blend to a smooth purée.

When the rice is nearly ready, add the diced and puréed red beets. Cook for 2–3 minutes until the rice is tender, then stir in the butter, cover and leave to stand for 1 minute. Season to taste, then spoon into bowls and serve scattered with the goats' cheese and dill.

quinoa, broad bean & avocado salad

THE SCIENCE BIT

Taking on regular brain exercises like sudoku and crossword puzzles will keep your brain young and active.

SERVES 4

Prep + cook time: 30 minutes

200 g (7 oz) quinoa, rinsed

800 ml (1 pint 8 fl oz) hot vegetable stock (see page 9 for homemade)

500 g (1 lb) podded fava beans

1 tablespoon cumin seeds

3 lemons

2 ripe avocados

2 garlic cloves, crushed

2 red chillies, finely chopped

200 g (7 oz) radishes, thickly sliced

small handful of chopped cilantro leaves

5 tablespoons extra-virgin olive oil

salt and pepper

Place the quinoa in a medium saucepan with the stock. Bring to the boil, reduce the heat and simmer for 10–12 minutes, uncovered, until most of the stock has been absorbed. Drain and leave to cool.

Meanwhile, cook the fava beans in a saucepan of boiling water for 1–2 minutes. Drain, then place in a bowl of cold water and leave to cool slightly. Drain again, slip off and discard the skins and set aside.

Heat a frying pan until hot and dry-fry the cumin seeds over a medium heat until lightly brown; remove from pan and leave to cool. Lightly crush the seeds.

Using a sharp knife, remove the peel and pith from the lemons. Holding them over a large bowl to catch the juice, cut into segments, discarding any seeds, and place the segments in the bowl.

Peel, pit and thickly slice the avocados, add to the bowl and toss in the lemon juice. Add the quinoa, beans, cumin seeds and the remaining ingredients, then season. Toss to mix well and serve.

sweet potato & red pepper soup

THE SCIENCE BIT

A large red pepper provides up to 75 per cent of your daily requirement of manganese, a mineral that helps build strong bones.

SERVES 4
Prep + cook time: 30 minutes

2 tablespoons vegetable oil
1 red onion, chopped
1 red pepper, cored, deseeded and
   chopped
550 g (1 lb 2 oz) sweet potatoes,
   peeled and chopped
¼ teaspoon ground cumin
8 cherry tomatoes
1.2 litres (2 pints) vegetable stock
   (see page 9 for homemade)
25 g (1 oz) creamed coconut,
   chopped
salt and pepper
natural yogurt and cilantro sprigs,
   to serve

Heat the oil in a saucepan over a medium heat, add the onion and pepper and cook for 3–4 minutes. Stir in the sweet potatoes, cumin and tomatoes, and cook for a further 2–3 minutes.

Pour in the stock, bring to the boil and simmer for 12 minutes. Stir in the creamed coconut and cook for a further 2–3 minutes. Blend the soup until smooth.

Season with salt and pepper and serve the soup topped with a dollop of natural yogurt and a sprig of cilantro.

Muscle weakening occurs with age, but you can counter this by dancing which is an easy – and fun – way to stimulate muscles while improving balance and flexibility.

zucchini, apple & clementine salad

THE SCIENCE BIT

Apples are a crisp, delicious way to keep joints healthy. They contain quercetin, which helps build collagen, a main component of cartilage.

SERVES 4–6

Prep + cook time: 35 minutes

2 zucchinis, halved and thinly sliced lengthways

1 crisp green or red apple, cored and thinly sliced

2–3 tablespoons olive oil

1 tablespoon runny honey

2 teaspoons fennel seeds

2 sweet clementines, peeled and pith removed

juice of 1 lemon

finely sliced rind of ½ preserved lemon

salt

Place the zucchinis and apple in a baking dish and spoon over the oil. Place in a preheated oven, 200°C (400°F) for about 15 minutes. Drizzle over the honey, then return to the oven and cook for a further 5–10 minutes until softened and slightly golden.

Meanwhile, dry-fry the fennel seeds in a small, heavy-based frying pan over a medium heat for 2–3 minutes until they emit a nutty aroma. Set aside.

Place the clementines on a plate to catch the juice and thinly slice into circles, removing any seeds. Arrange the slices in a serving dish and spoon the roasted zucchini and apple on top.

Stir any clementine juice into the roasting juices in the baking dish. Add the lemon juice and season with a little salt. Drizzle over the salad and scatter with the toasted fennel seeds and preserved lemon rind. Serve warm or at room temperature.

sweetcorn cakes with avocado salsa

THE SCIENCE BIT

The tangy avocado salsa in this recipe is full of powerful antioxidants and anti-inflammatories to combat joint pain and muscle soreness.

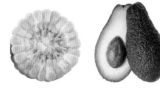

SERVES 4
Prep + cook time: 30 minutes

500 g (1 lb) fresh sweetcorn kernels
4 scallions, finely sliced
2 eggs
5 tablespoons finely chopped
   cilantro leaves, plus extra
   to garnish
125 g (4 oz) plain flour
1 teaspoon baking powder
salt and pepper
vegetable oil, for frying

avocado salsa
2 ripe avocados, peeled, pitted and
   finely diced
4 tablespoons each of chopped mint
   and cilantro leaves
2 tablespoons lime juice
2 tablespoons finely chopped
   red onion
½ teaspoon Tabasco sauce

Place three-quarters of the sweetcorn kernels along with the scallions, eggs, cilantro, flour and baking powder in a food processor and whizz until combined. Season well and transfer to a large bowl. Add the remaining sweetcorn kernels and mix well.

Heat 1 tablespoon of vegetable oil in a large nonstick frying pan over a medium–high heat. When the oil is hot, drop heaped tablespoons of the mixture into the pan and cook in batches for 1 minute on each side.

Drain the sweetcorn cakes on kitchen paper and keep warm in a low oven while making the rest of the cakes.

Make the avocado salsa. Place all the ingredients in a bowl and stir very gently to combine.

Serve the warm sweetcorn cakes accompanied by the tangy avocado salsa and garnished with cilantro leaves.

butternut squash, carrot & mango tagine

THE SCIENCE BIT

Love your heart by eating orange veggies like the squash and carrots in this tagine as they're packed full of carotenoids.

SERVES 4

Prep + cook time: 55 minutes

2 tablespoons olive oil
1 large onion, cut into large chunks
3 garlic cloves, finely chopped
1 butternut squash, about 875 g
 (1¾ lb) peeled, deseeded and cubed
2 small carrots, cut into thick batons
½ × 2.5 cm (1 inch) cinnamon stick
½ teaspoon turmeric
¼ teaspoon cayenne pepper
 (optional)
½ teaspoon ground cumin
1 teaspoon paprika
pinch of saffron threads
1 tablespoon tomato purée
750 ml (1¼ pints) hot vegetable stock
 (see page 9 for homemade)
1 mango, peeled, pitted and cut into
 2.5 cm (1 inch) chunks
salt and pepper
2 tablespoons chopped cilantro, to
 garnish

Heat the oil in a large, heavy-based saucepan over a medium heat, add the onion and cook for 5 minutes or until beginning to soften. Add the garlic, squash, carrots and spices and fry gently for a further 5 minutes.

Stir in the tomato purée, then pour in the stock and season with salt and pepper to taste. Cover and simmer gently for 20–25 minutes or until the vegetables are tender. Stir in the mango and simmer gently for a further 5 minutes.

Spoon the tagine into serving bowls and sprinkle with the cilantro.

It's good to laugh — studies suggest it can lower stress hormones, decrease inflammation in your arteries and raise your levels of "good" cholesterol.

parsley, tomato & pomegranate molasses salad

THE SCIENCE BIT

Eating plenty of tomatoes has been linked to a decrease in "bad" cholesterol levels and risk of stroke.

SERVES 4
Prep + cook time: 20 minutes

2 tomatoes
large bunch of flat leaf parsley,
　roughly chopped
2 red onions, finely sliced
2 teaspoons cilantro seeds
finely sliced rind of 1 preserved
　lemon
2 tablespoons pomegranate
　molasses
salt and pepper

Place the tomatoes in a heatproof bowl and pour over boiling water to cover. Leave for 1–2 minutes, then drain, cut a cross at the stem end of each tomato and peel off the skins. Cut into quarters, remove the seeds and roughly chop the flesh. Place in a serving bowl and add the parsley and onions.

Dry-fry the cilantro seeds in a small, heavy-based frying pan over a medium heat for 2 minutes until they emit a nutty aroma. Using a pestle and mortar, lightly crush the seeds. Add to the tomato mixture with the preserved lemon rind.

Pour over the pomegranate molasses and season well. Gently toss together before serving.

A North African speciality, preserved lemons are made by preserving whole lemons in a mixture of salt and lemon juice or oil. Rinse the rind well before using it.

spicy soy bean & noodle salad

THE SCIENCE BIT

The soy beans in this Asian-style salad are low in saturated fat and are an excellent source of high-quality protein.

SERVES 4
Prep + cook time: 25 minutes

250 g (8 oz) frozen podded soy beans
250 g (8 oz) dried soba noodles
6 scallions, thinly sliced diagonally
2 tablespoons sesame seeds
3 cm (1 inch) piece of fresh ginger
1 red chilli, finely chopped
1 tablespoon toasted sesame oil
3 tablespoons mirin
3 tablespoons light soy sauce
1 teaspoon clear honey
salt
chopped cilantro leaves, to garnish

Cook the fava beans in a saucepan of boiling water for 1–2 minutes. Drain, then place in a bowl of cold water and leave to cool slightly. Drain again, slip off and discard the skins and set aside.

Cook the noodles in a large saucepan of lightly salted boiling water for 4–5 minutes, or according to the noodle packet instructions. Drain well, then return to the pan and add the scallions and soy beans. Cover and keep warm.

Heat a frying pan until hot, add the sesame seeds and dry-fry over a medium heat until lightly golden, then remove from the pan and set aside.

Peel and grate the ginger into a bowl, then stir in the remaining ingredients and mix well. Pour the dressing over the noodle mixture and toss to mix well.

Spoon into bowls, scatter over the sesame seeds and chopped cilantro and serve.

vegetable biryani

THE SCIENCE BIT

This recipe contains an array of heart-healthy ingredients including potatoes and garlic to lower blood pressure and nuts to reduce "bad" cholesterol.

SERVES 4

Prep + cook time: 30 minutes

250 g (8 oz) long-grain rice
2 tablespoons olive oil
3 carrots, chopped
2 medium potatoes, chopped
2.5 cm (1 inch) piece of fresh ginger, peeled and grated
2 garlic cloves, crushed
200 g (7 oz) cauliflower florets
125 g (4 oz) green beans, halved
1 tablespoon hot curry paste
1 teaspoon turmeric
1 teaspoon ground cinnamon
250 g (8 oz) natural yogurt
40 g (1½ oz) raisins
75 g (3 oz) toasted cashew nuts and 2 tablespoons chopped cilantro leaves, to serve

Cook the rice according to the packet instructions and drain.

Meanwhile, heat the oil in a saucepan, add the carrots, potato, ginger and garlic and fry for 10 minutes until soft, adding a little water if the potatoes begin to stick.

Stir in the cauliflower, beans, curry paste, turmeric and cinnamon and cook for 1 minute. Stir in the yogurt and raisins.

Pile the rice on top of the vegetables, cover and cook over a low heat for 10 minutes, checking it isn't sticking to the pan.

Serve the biryani sprinkled with the cashew nuts and cilantro.

One serving of cauliflower contains over 70 per cent of the vitamin C we need each day and it contains sulforaphane which improves blood pressure for better cardiovascular health.

ANTI-AGEING

eggplant pâté

THE SCIENCE BIT

Nanusin — which gives eggplants their rich purple color — may slow the development of Alzheimer's disease by preventing free radicals from damaging neurons.

SERVES 2

Prep + cook time: 50 minutes

2 eggplants, cubed
2 garlic cloves, sliced
2 tablespoons olive oil
1 teaspoon cumin seeds
pinch of chili flakes
1 tablespoon chopped cilantro
salt and pepper
toasted pitta bread, to serve

Put the eggplants in a baking tin and add the garlic. Drizzle over the oil and then sprinkle over the cumin seeds and chili flakes. Season well with salt and pepper.

Cook in a preheated oven, 200°C (400°F) for 35–40 minutes until tender and golden.

Transfer the mixture to a food processor or blender and process for a few seconds so that the mixture still has some texture. Leave to cool, then stir through the chopped cilantro. Serve with toasted pitta bread.

Aside from adding flavor to this Middle Eastern-inspired pâté, garlic contains manganese, vitamins B6 and C and selenium.

broccoli & baby corn stir-fry with oyster sauce

THE SCIENCE BIT

Evidence suggests a compound known as NMN – nicotinamide mononucleotide – found in broccoli, cabbage and avocado can help slow the physical signs of ageing.

SERVES 4

Prep + cook time: 30 minutes

2 teaspoons sesame seed oil
2 garlic cloves, thinly sliced
1 tablespoon peeled, grated and chopped fresh ginger
1 red chilli, deseeded and finely chopped
2 scallions, thickly sliced
125 g (4 oz) baby corn
300 g (10 oz) purple sprouting broccoli stems
4 tablespoons vegetarian oyster sauce
2 tablespoons light soy sauce
2 teaspoons toasted sesame seeds

ginger & lemongrass rice
1 lemongrass stalk
300 g (10 oz) Thai jasmine rice
1 tablespoon grated and chopped fresh ginger
1 teaspoon salt
750 ml (1¼ pints) water

Make the ginger and lemongrass rice by removing the outer leaves of the lemon grass and finely slicing the tender heart. Rinse the rice 2–3 times. Place in a saucepan with the lemongrass, ginger and salt. Add the measurement water and bring to the boil. Reduce the heat, cover the pan with a tight-fitting lid and simmer gently for 14–16 minutes or until the rice is sticky and tender and the water is absorbed. Set aside.

Heat the oil in a large wok over a medium heat, then add garlic, ginger, chilli and scallions and stir-fry for 30 seconds. Add the baby corn and broccoli and stir-fry for 3–4 minutes until almost tender, then stir in the oyster sauce and light soy sauce and simmer gently for 30 seconds.

Remove the stir-fry from the heat and serve with the ginger and lemongrass rice with the sesame seeds sprinkled over.

avocado, pepper & olive salad

THE SCIENCE BIT

Antioxidants found in avocados help to combat free radicals to slow down the ageing process of your skin.

SERVES 4
Prep + cook time: 10 minutes

1 tablespoon sesame seeds
2 ripe avocados, peeled, pitted
  and chopped
juice of 1 lime
1 red pepper, cored, deseeded and
  chopped
1 yellow pepper, cored, deseeded
  and chopped
½ cucumber, finely chopped
2 carrots, chopped
2 tomatoes, chopped
4 scallions, sliced
10 pitted black olives, halved
1 romaine lettuce, roughly torn
1 tablespoon chopped mint

Heat a nonstick frying pan over a medium-low heat and dry-fry the sesame seeds for 2 minutes, stirring frequently, until golden brown and toasted. Set aside.

Meanwhile, place the avocados in a large bowl and toss with the lime juice to prevent discoloration. Gently toss together with the remaining ingredients except the sesame seeds.

Sprinkle the salad with the toasted sesame seeds and serve.

Vitamin C, beta-carotene, fiber, folic acid and potassium in romaine lettuce make it an excellent choice for healthy salads.

ANTI-AGEING

red cabbage & red beets lentils

THE SCIENCE BIT

Red beets and red cabbage are chock-full of antioxidants which not only protect against cancer, but help to ward off wrinkles too.

SERVES 2

Prep + cook time: 30 minutes

2 tablespoons olive or vegetable oil
½ small red cabbage, thinly sliced
2 scallions, sliced, plus extra
  to garnish
1 raw red beet, coarsely grated
1 teaspoon ground cumin
300 g (10 oz) canned green lentils,
  rinsed and drained
salt and pepper
natural or Greek yogurt, to serve

Heat the oil in a saucepan and cook the red cabbage and scallions over a medium heat for about 5 minutes until just beginning to soften. Stir in the red beet, then cover and cook for a further 8–10 minutes, stirring occasionally, until the vegetables are tender.

Sprinkle over the ground cumin and stir over the heat for a minute, then add the lentils and heat until hot. Season to taste, then spoon into dishes and serve with a dollop of yogurt and extra sliced scallion.

If you get more of your protein from vegetable or plant-based foods, studies have shown that you will live longer. Lower rates of cardiovascular disease are linked to a diet that is rich in legumes, such as lentils.

chilled avocado soup

THE SCIENCE BIT

This refreshing soup is based on creamy avocados which are high in many essential vitamins and minerals, especially vitamin E, a powerful antioxidant.

SERVES 4
Prep time: 10 minutes + chilling

4 large ripe avocados, peeled and pitted
juice of 1 lime
½ red chilli, deseeded and diced
900 ml (1½ pints) vegetable stock, chilled (see page 9 for homemade)
2 scallions, finely sliced
½ red pepper, cored, deseeded and diced
¼ cucumber, diced
1 tablespoon cilantro leaves
2 tablespoons olive oil
2 teaspoons lemon juice
2 tablespoons pumpkin seeds, toasted
salt and pepper
8 ice cubes, to serve

Place the avocados, lime juice and chilli in a food processor or blender and blend with the chilled stock until smooth. Season to taste with salt and pepper and chill for 15 minutes.

Meanwhile, mix together the remaining ingredients.

Place 2 ice cubes in each of 4 shallow bowls, and pour over the soup.

Sprinkle over the salsa and serve.

To toast the pumpkin seeds, brush a frying pan with a very small amount of vegetable or olive oil and place over a medium heat. Add the pumpkin seeds, stirring frequently, until they have expanded and browned.

mushrooms with goats' cheese & arugula

THE SCIENCE BIT

Keeping stress levels down, eating a varied diet and exercising more will all help boost your immune system naturally.

SERVES 4

Prep + cook time: 30 minutes

500 g (1 lb) new potatoes, halved
3 tablespoons olive oil
200 g (7 oz) portobello mushrooms
2 tablespoons chopped thyme
6 garlic cloves, unpeeled
50 g (2 oz) soft goats' cheese
125 g (4 oz) cherry tomatoes
25 g (1 oz) toasted pine nuts
75 g (3 oz) arugula leaves, to serve
salt and pepper

Toss the potatoes with 2 tablespoons olive oil and place in a large, shallow roasting tin. Place in a preheated oven, 220°C (425°F) for 15 minutes, turning once.

Add the mushrooms, stem side up, thyme and garlic to the tin, drizzle over the remaining oil and season well. Place a little goats' cheese on each mushroom and return to the oven for a further 5 minutes.

Add the cherry tomatoes and return to the oven for a further 5 minutes more until the potatoes and mushrooms are cooked through. Scatter over the pine nuts and serve with the arugula.

Mushrooms are one of the few foods that contain vitamin D. Vitamin D helps to regulate the amount of calcium and phosphate in the body to keep bones, teeth and muscles healthy.

broccoli & mushrooms in black bean sauce

THE SCIENCE BIT
Superfood broccoli contains choline which helps to keep all the cells in your body functioning properly.

SERVES 4
Prep + cook time: 20 minutes

1 tablespoon sunflower oil
1.5 cm (¾ in) piece of fresh ginger, peeled and sliced
200 g (7 oz) small broccoli florets
200 g (7 oz) shiitake mushrooms
6 scallions, sliced
1 red pepper, cored, deseeded and sliced
300 ml (½ pint) vegetable stock
500 g (1 lb) fresh egg noodles
2 tablespoons light soy sauce
1 tablespoon cornflour mixed to a paste with 2 tablespoons water

black bean sauce
1 tablespoon fermented salted black beans, rinsed well
1 tablespoon light soy sauce
2 garlic cloves, crushed
1 red chilli, deseeded and chopped
1 tablespoon Shaohsing rice wine

Place all the ingredients for the black bean sauce in a food processor or blender, blend until fairly smooth and set aside.

Heat a wok over high heat and add the oil. When smoking, add the ginger and stir-fry for a few seconds. Add the broccoli and stir-fry for a further 2–3 minutes.

Add the mushrooms, scallions and red pepper and stir-fry for 2–3 minutes.

Tip in the black bean sauce and vegetable stock and bring to a simmer. Cook for 2–3 minutes until tender.

Meanwhile, cook the noodles according to the packet instructions, drain and keep warm.

Season with soy sauce to taste, mix in the blended cornflour paste and cook to thicken for 1 minute. Serve immediately with the egg noodles.

okra & coconut stew

THE SCIENCE BIT

Getting enough vitamin C is a great way to bolster your immune system. Low-calorie, high-fiber okra is packed with vitamin C.

SERVES 4
Prep + cook time: 55 minutes

375 g (12 oz) okra
4 tablespoons vegetable oil
2 onions, chopped
2 green peppers, cored, deseeded
  and cut into chunks
3 celery sticks, thinly sliced
3 garlic cloves, crushed
4 teaspoons Cajun spice blend
½ teaspoon ground turmeric
300 ml (½ pint) vegetable stock
  (see page 9 for homemade)
400 ml (14 fl oz) can coconut milk
200 g (7 oz) frozen sweetcorn
juice of 1 lime
4 tablespoons chopped cilantro
salt and pepper

Trim the stalk ends from the okra and cut the pods into 1.5 cm (¾ inch) lengths.

Heat 2 tablespoons of the oil in a large deep-sided frying pan or shallow flameproof casserole and fry the okra for 5 minutes. Lift out with a slotted spoon onto a plate.

Add the remaining oil to the pan and very gently fry the onions, peppers and celery, stirring frequently, for 10 minutes until softened but not browned. Add the garlic, spice blend and turmeric and cook for 1 minute.

Pour in the stock and coconut milk and bring to the boil. Reduce the heat, cover and cook gently for 10 minutes. Return the okra to the pan with the sweetcorn, lime juice and cilantro and cook for a further 10 minutes. Season to taste with salt and pepper and serve.

Thai veg salad

THE SCIENCE BIT

Sprouting your own seeds is a thrifty way to a healthy diet. Home-grown sprouts, such as alfalfa, have more vitamins than shop-bought versions.

SERVES 4

Prep + cook time: 15 minutes
  + cooling

250 g (8 oz) cherry tomatoes,
  quartered
½ cucumber, thinly sliced
1 green papaya or green mango
1 large red chilli, deseeded and thinly
  sliced
150 g (5 oz) bean sprouts
4 scallions, trimmed and thinly sliced
small handful each of Thai basil, mint
  and cilantro leaves
4 tablespoons unsalted peanuts,
  roughly chopped

chilli dressing

2 tablespoons sweet chilli sauce
2 tablespoons light soy sauce
2 tablespoons lime juice
2 tablespoons lime marmalade

Make the dressing. Put all the ingredients in a small saucepan and warm over a low heat, stirring, until combined. Leave to cool.

Put the tomatoes, cucumber, papaya or mango, chilli, bean sprouts, scallions and herbs in a bowl. Add the dressing and toss well. Transfer to a platter. Sprinkle over the peanuts and serve immediately.

Start your meal with a glass of water. Several studies have linked drinking water before eating with greater weight loss.

roast root vegetable soup

THE SCIENCE BIT

Research indicates that soup can make you feel fuller for longer, so it's a great lunchtime choice that will stop mid-afternoon snacking.

SERVES 6

Prep + cook time: 1 hour
  15 minutes

4 carrots, chopped
2 parsnips, chopped
olive oil, for spraying
1 leek, trimmed and finely chopped
1.2 litres (2 pints) vegetable stock
  (see page 9 for homemade)
2 teaspoons thyme leaves
salt and pepper
thyme sprigs, to garnish

Place the carrots and parsnips in a roasting tin, spray lightly with olive oil and season with salt and pepper. Roast in a preheated oven, 200°C (400°F) for 1 hour or until the vegetables are very soft.

Meanwhile, 20 minutes before the vegetables have finished roasting, put the leeks in a large saucepan with the stock and 1 teaspoon of the thyme. Cover the pan and simmer for 20 minutes.

Transfer the roasted root vegetables to a blender or food processor and blend, adding a little of the stock if necessary. Transfer to the stock saucepan and season to taste. Add the remaining thyme, stir and simmer for 5 minutes to reheat.

Ladle into bowls and serve garnished with the thyme sprigs.

Carrots are a good source of beta-carotene, calcium, phosphorus and magnesium.

zucchini, tomato & mint curry

THE SCIENCE BIT

The zucchinis, onions and tomatoes in this colorful curry are low in calories and provide vitamins A, B6, C and E.

SERVES 4

Prep + cook time: 40 minutes

2 tablespoons olive oil

2 onions, finely sliced

4 zucchinis, cut into 1 cm (½ inch) cubes

2 x 400 g (13 oz) cans peeled plum tomatoes

2 garlic cloves, crushed

1 teaspoon mild chilli powder

¼ teaspoon ground turmeric

2 teaspoons dried mint

salt and pepper

small handful of finely chopped mint leaves, to garnish

Heat the oil in a large heavy-based saucepan, add the onion and cook over a medium-low heat, stirring occasionally, for 6–8 minutes until softened. Add the zucchinis and cook, stirring occasionally, for a further 5–6 minutes until tender.

Increase the heat to medium, add the tomatoes and garlic and cook for 10–12 minutes until the sauce is thickened. Stir in the chilli powder, turmeric and mint and cook for a further 2–3 minutes. Season well.

Ladle into bowls and serve scattered with the chopped mint leaves.

There is evidence that being in a colder environment can help increase our levels of brown fat cells which burn energy, which is a good incentive to turn down the heating and head outside.

WEIGHT LOSS

spicy lentils & chickpeas

THE SCIENCE BIT

The protein and fiber in diet-friendly chickpeas and lentils delay stomach emptying so you feel fuller for longer.

SERVES 4

Prep + cook time: 50 minutes

1 tablespoon groundnut oil

1 onion, finely chopped

2 garlic cloves, thinly sliced

2 celery sticks, diced

1 green pepper, cored, deseeded and chopped

150 g (5 oz) red lentils, rinsed

2 teaspoons garam masala

1 teaspoon cumin seeds

½ teaspoon hot chilli powder

1 teaspoon ground cilantro

2 tablespoons tomato purée

750 ml (1¼ pints) hot vegetable stock (see page 9 for homemade)

400 g (13 oz) can chickpeas, rinsed and drained

salt and pepper

2 tablespoons chopped cilantro, to garnish

boiled brown rice, to serve

Heat the oil in a heavy-based saucepan over a medium heat, add the onion, garlic, celery and green pepper and fry gently for 10–12 minutes or until softened and beginning to color.

Stir in the lentils and spices and cook for 2–3 minutes, stirring frequently. Add the tomato purée, stock and chickpeas and bring to the boil. Reduce the heat, cover and simmer gently for about 20 minutes or until the lentils collapse. Season with salt and pepper to taste.

Ladle into bowls and sprinkle with the cilantro. Serve immediately with boiled brown rice.

A Canadian study found that eating one serving of chickpeas, lentils or beans daily can reduce your "bad" LDL levels by 5 per cent.

DETOX

melon, mint & strawberry smoothie

THE SCIENCE BIT

Smoothies, which provide your body with essential nutrients without overloading it, are ideal choices for detox days.

SERVES 4
Prep time: 10 minutes

1 small watermelon, peeled, deseeded and chopped
14–16 strawberries, hulled
12 mint leaves
small handful of ice

Place all the ingredients in a blender or food processor and blend until smooth.

Pour into tall glasses and serve immediately.

Summer favorite, strawberries are an excellent source of vitamins C and K and also provide fiber, folic acid, potassium and manganese.

pink grapefruit & fennel salad

THE SCIENCE BIT

Low in calories and full of fiber, vitamin C and water, grapefruit has been shown to boost the metabolism.

SERVES 4
Prep + cook time: 30 minutes

1 fennel bulb
1 tablespoon olive oil
juice of ½ lemon
1 scant teaspoon cumin seeds, crushed
2 pink grapefruit
1 scant teaspoon salt
2–3 scallions, finely sliced
1 tablespoon black olives, pitted

Cut the base off the fennel and remove the outer layers. Cut in half lengthways and in half horizontally, then finely slice with the grain. Place in a bowl and toss with the oil, lemon juice and cumin seeds. Leave to marinate for 20 minutes.

Meanwhile, using a sharp knife, remove the peel and pith from the grapefruit. Holding the grapefruit over a bowl to catch the juice, cut down between the membranes and remove the segments. Cut each segment in half, place in the bowl and sprinkle with the salt. Leave to stand for 5 minutes to draw out the sweet juices.

Add the fennel to the grapefruit and mix in the scallions. Serve topped with the olives.

An average fennel bulb contains only 73 calories, a trace of fat, 3 grams of protein and provides around a quarter of your daily requirement of dietary fiber.

DETOX

melon, olive, green bean & feta salad

THE SCIENCE BIT
Consisting of 92 per cent water and full of vitamins and minerals, watermelon is a great detox choice to flush out an overworked system.

SERVES 4
Prep + cook time: 20 minutes

300 g (10 oz) green beans, halved
1 red onion
juice of 2 limes
1.5 kg (3 lb) watermelon
250 g (8 oz) feta cheese
100 g (3½ oz) black olives, pitted
1 bunch flat leaf parsley, roughly
  chopped
1 bunch mint leaves, roughly
  chopped
5 tablespoons extra-virgin olive oil
salt and pepper

Blanch the green beans in a saucepan of boiling water for 3 minutes. Drain, refresh under cold water and set aside.

Halve the red onion and cut into thin slices. Place in a small bowl with the drained beans and the lime juice and allow to steep. Season with salt.

Remove the rind and pips from the watermelon and cut into bite-sized pieces. Cut the feta into similarly sized pieces and put them both into a large, wide, shallow bowl or serving dish.

Add the red onions and beans, along with their juices, to the bowl or serving dish. Scatter over the olives and herbs. Season well, drizzle with oil and serve at room temperature.

Brushing with a body brush or mitt stimulates your body to get rid of toxins. It improves circulation, speeds up lymphatic drainage and gives you a glow.

VEGETARIAN RECIPES FOR RECOVERY AND RECUPERATION

introduction

Vitamin C-rich tomatoes to beat the winter sniffles, walnuts to help you sleep, tummy-calming bananas, beans for blood pressure regulation, and much more – the recipes in this chapter offer a host of wonderfully healing benefits to help you get better and stay better.

Alongside the health-enhancing benefits of eating well, it is important to consider other aspects of your lifestyle. Regular exercise is key – guidelines advise that you should try to be active daily and should aim for 150 minutes of moderate aerobic activity every week. Exercise needn't involve a long workout at the gym – a brisk walk in the fresh air, a swim or a bike ride, even pushing the lawnmower around the garden will all build a stronger mind and body.

chickpea & tomato linguine

THE SCIENCE BIT

Foods rich in zinc, like the chickpeas in this recipe, help keep your immune system in tip-top shape to fight colds and flu.

SERVES 4

Prep + cook time: 20 minutes

2 tablespoons olive oil

1 onion, chopped

2 garlic cloves, crushed

1 celery stick, sliced

400 g (13 oz) can chopped tomatoes

175 g (6 oz) baby spinach leaves

400 g (13 oz) can chickpeas, rinsed and drained

350 g (11½ oz) linguine

10 basil leaves, torn

50 g (2 oz) grated Parmesan-style cheese, to serve

Heat the oil in a large saucepan, add the onion, garlic and celery and cook for 3–4 minutes until softened. Add the tomatoes and bring to the boil, then reduce the heat and simmer for 10 minutes. Stir in the spinach and chickpeas and cook until the spinach is wilted.

Meanwhile, cook the pasta in a saucepan of boiling water for 6–8 minutes, or according to packet instructions, until al dente. Drain, then add to the tomato sauce with the basil and toss together.

Serve sprinkled with the cheese.

While vitamin C won't stop you getting a cold, it can reduce the severity, making this dish, which is crammed with vitamin C from the tomatoes, spinach, onion and basil, one to turn to when the sniffles start.

pumpkin, orange & star anise soup

THE SCIENCE BIT

Cold-proof your immune system by opting for foods that are high in vitamin A, like the pumpkin in this soup.

SERVES 6

Prep + cook time: 1 hour 15 minutes

25 g (1 oz) butter
1 onion, roughly chopped
1 small pumpkin, about 1.5 kg (3 lb), quartered, deseeded, peeled and diced
2 small oranges, rind removed with a zester, juice squeezed
1 litre (1¾ pints) vegetable stock (see page 9 for homemade)
3 whole star anise or similar amount in pieces, plus extra to garnish
salt and pepper
crushed black peppercorns, to garnish (optional)

Heat the butter in a large saucepan, add the onion and fry gently for 5 minutes until softened. Add the pumpkin, toss in the butter and fry for 5 minutes, stirring.

Mix in the orange rind and juice, the stock and star anise. Season and bring to the boil. Cover and simmer for 30 minutes, stirring occasionally until the pumpkin is soft. Remove the star anise and reserve.

Blend until smooth and adjust the seasoning.

Ladle the soup into bowls and garnish each bowl with a whole star anise and a sprinkling of black pepper, or a slice of spiced orange and chilli butter.

Comforting soup offers an easy way to digest the essential nutrients that your body needs when you have a cold.

Provençal vegetable stew

THE SCIENCE BIT

This stew contains fennel which is a natural expectorant and can help clear chest congestion, plus vitamin C-rich tomatoes and red pepper.

SERVES 4

Prep + cook time: 1 hour 10 minutes

4 tablespoons extra-virgin olive oil, plus extra for drizzling

1 large red onion, sliced

4 garlic cloves, chopped

2 teaspoons ground cilantro

1 tablespoon chopped thyme

1 fennel bulb, trimmed and sliced

1 red pepper, cored, deseeded and sliced

500 g (1 lb) vine-ripened tomatoes, diced

300 ml (½ pint) vegetable stock (see page 9 for homemade)

125 g (4 oz) Niçoise olives

2 tablespoons chopped parsley

slices of crusty bread

salt and pepper

Heat the oil in a large saucepan, add the onion, garlic, cilantro and thyme and cook over a medium heat, stirring frequently, for 5 minutes until the onion is softened. Add the fennel and red pepper and cook, stirring frequently, for 10 minutes until softened.

Stir in the tomatoes, stock and salt and pepper. Bring to the boil, then reduce the heat, cover and simmer gently for 30 minutes. Stir in the olives and parsley and simmer, uncovered, for a further 10 minutes.

Meanwhile, heat a ridged griddle pan until hot. Add the bread slices and cook until toasted and charred on both sides. Drizzle liberally with oil.

Serve the stew hot with the toasted bread.

Sometimes called "Russian penicillin", garlic has a long history of use as an infection fighter against colds, viruses, bacteria and fungi.

COLDS

veg-stuffed roasted peppers

THE SCIENCE BIT
A medium red pepper provides nearly 200 per cent of your daily requirement of vitamin C and about 25 per cent of vitamin A.

SERVES 4
Prep + cook time: 30 minutes

2 red peppers, halved, cored and deseeded
2 yellow peppers, halved, cored and deseeded
1 small red onion, cut into 8 wedges
2 runner beans, trimmed and cut into small batons
1 zucchini, sliced
3 garlic cloves, sliced
2 tablespoons extra-virgin olive oil
1 teaspoon cumin seeds
salt and pepper
100 g (3½ oz) feta or goats' cheese, to serve (optional)

Place the pepper halves, cut side up, in a roasting tin and divide the vegetables and garlic among them.

Sprinkle with the oil and cumin seeds and season with salt and pepper. Place in a preheated oven, 190°C (375°F) for 25 minutes until tender. Sprinkle with feta or goats' cheese, to serve, if liked.

It's important to keep up hydration levels when you have a cold. Herbal teas and other hot liquids help thin mucus and expel it from the body.

banana & buttermilk pancakes

THE SCIENCE BIT

Bananas are a great source of potassium that holds on to water to decrease dehydration and soothe hangover headaches.

SERVES 4
Prep + cook time: 30 minutes

125 g (4 oz) plain flour
pinch of salt
1 teaspoon baking powder
200 ml (7 fl oz) buttermilk
1 egg
2 small bananas, thinly sliced
1 tablespoon vegetable oil

to serve
1 banana, sliced
25 g (1 oz) pecan nuts, chopped
2 tablespoons maple syrup

Sift the flour, salt and baking powder together into a large bowl, then make a well in the center.

Beat the buttermilk and egg together in a jug, add to the well and gradually beat in the flour mixture from around the sides to make a smooth batter. Stir in the sliced bananas.

Heat a large nonstick frying pan over a medium heat. Dip a scrunched-up piece of kitchen paper into the oil and use to wipe over the pan. Drop 3 large tablespoonfuls of the batter into the pan to make 3 pancakes, spreading the batter out slightly with the spoon. Cook for 2–3 minutes until bubbles start to appear on the surface and the underside is golden brown, then flip over and cook for a further 2 minutes. Transfer the pancakes to a baking sheet and keep warm in a low oven while you repeat with the remaining oil and batter.

Serve 3 pancakes per person, topped with the extra sliced banana, sprinkled with the chopped nuts and drizzled with the maple syrup.

Moroccan baked eggs

THE SCIENCE BIT

Eggs provide energy to help you get going in the morning and also contain cysteine to break down the toxin that causes hangovers.

SERVES 4

Prep + cook time: 35 minutes

1 tablespoon olive oil
1 onion, chopped
2 garlic cloves, sliced
1 teaspoon ras el hanout
¼ teaspoon ground cinnamon
1 teaspoon ground cilantro
800 g (1 lb 12 oz) can cherry tomatoes
4 tablespoons chopped cilantro
4 eggs
salt and pepper
crusty bread, to serve

Preheat the oven to 220°C (425°F). Heat the olive oil in a frying pan over a medium heat, add the onion and garlic and cook for 6–7 minutes or until softened and lightly golden, stirring occasionally.

Stir in the spices and cook for a further minute, then add the cherry tomatoes. Season generously with salt and pepper, then simmer gently for 8–10 minutes. Scatter over 3 tablespoons of the cilantro.

Divide the tomato mixture into 4 individual ovenproof dishes, then crack an egg into each dish. Cook in the oven for 8–10 minutes until the egg is set but the yolks are still slightly runny. Cook for a further 2–3 minutes if you prefer the eggs to be cooked through.

Serve scattered with the remaining cilantro and plenty of crusty bread on the side.

HANGOVERS

red pepper &
ginger soup

THE SCIENCE BIT

Soup is a great option if you're
feeling too queasy for solid food
and ginger is a well-known
remedy for nausea.

SERVES 4

Prep + cook time: I hour + cooling

3 red peppers, halved, cored and
  deseeded
I red onion, quartered
2 garlic cloves
I teaspoon olive oil
5 cm (2 inch) piece of fresh ginger,
  peeled and grated
I teaspoon ground cumin
I teaspoon ground cilantro
I large potato, chopped
900 ml (1½ pints) vegetable stock
  (see page 9 for homemade)
4 tablespoons fromage frais
salt and pepper

Put peppers, onion and garlic in a nonstick roasting
tin. Roast in a preheated oven, 200°C (400°F) for
40 minutes or until the peppers have blistered and
the onion and garlic are soft. If the onion quarters
start to brown too much, cover them with the
pepper halves and continue cooking.

Meanwhile, heat the oil in a large saucepan and
fry the ginger, cumin and cilantro over a low heat
for 5 minutes until soft. Add the potato, stir well and
season to taste. Add the stock, cover the pan and
simmer for 30 minutes.

Place the roasted peppers in a food bag, seal and
leave to cool. Add the onions to the potato mixture
and squeeze the garlic pulp from the skins into the
pan. Remove the skins from the peppers and add
all but one half to the soup. Simmer for 5 minutes.
Blend the soup until smooth.

Ladle the soup into bowls. Slice the remaining
pepper half and place the strips on top of the soup
with a spoonful of fromage frais.

asparagus & snow peas stir-fry

THE SCIENCE BIT

Researchers found that amino acids in asparagus help the body metabolize alcohol more quickly and protect liver cells at the same time.

SERVES 4
Prep + cook time: 20 minutes

2 tablespoons vegetable oil
100 g (3½ oz) fresh ginger, peeled and thinly shredded
2 large garlic cloves, thinly sliced
4 scallions, diagonally sliced
250 g (8 oz) thin asparagus spears, cut into 3 cm (1¼ inch) lengths
150 g (5 oz) snow peas, cut in half diagonally
150 g (5 oz) bean sprouts
3 tablespoons light soy sauce
steamed rice and extra soy sauce, to serve (optional)

Heat a large wok until it is smoking then add the oil. Stir-fry the ginger and garlic for 30 seconds, add the scallions and cook for a further 30 seconds. Add the asparagus and cook, stirring frequently, for another 3–4 minutes.

Add the snow peas and cook for 2–3 minutes until the vegetables are still crunchy but beginning to soften. Finally, add the bean sprouts and toss in the hot oil for 1–2 minutes before pouring in the soy sauce and removing from the heat.

Serve immediately with steamed rice and extra soy sauce, if liked.

Using a spoon is the easiest way to peel ginger. It scrapes away the skin but doesn't take any of the flesh with it. A spoon is also handy for getting into all those nooks and crannies.

crispy tortillas with hummus

THE SCIENCE BIT

Chickpeas are high in an amino acid called tryptophan, which has natural sedative qualities to lull you to sleep.

SERVES 4

Prep + cook time: 15 minutes

4 small wheat tortillas
1 tablespoon olive oil

hummus
410 g (13½ oz) can chickpeas, rinsed and drained
1 garlic clove, chopped
4–6 tablespoons natural yogurt
2 tablespoons lemon juice
1 tablespoon cilantro leaves, chopped
salt and pepper
paprika, to sprinkle
lemon wedges and olives, to serve

Cut each tortilla into 8 triangles, place on a baking sheet and brush with a little oil. Cook in a preheated oven, 200°C (400°F) for 10–12 minutes, until golden and crisp. Remove from the oven.

Meanwhile, put the chickpeas, garlic, yogurt and lemon juice in a bowl and mix really well until smooth and mushy. Sprinkle with salt and pepper, stir in the cilantro and sprinkle with paprika. Serve with the warm tortillas, lemon wedges and olives.

Avoid sugary foods if you are having trouble sleeping. An excess of sugar before bed can cause a spike in your blood-sugar levels which may disrupt your sleep.

INSOMNIA

baked spiced
bananas

Bananas are an excellent
source of magnesium and
potassium, to relax overstressed
muscles. They also contain
tryptophan for a good
night's rest.

SERVES 4
Prep + cook time: 20 minutes

4 ripe bananas, sliced lengthways
butter, for greasing
1 teaspoon ground allspice
½ teaspoon ground nutmeg
juice of 1 lemon
50 g (2 oz) flaked almonds
3 knobs of stem ginger, diced
200 g (7 oz) natural yogurt

Place the bananas in a lightly greased ovenproof
dish. Sprinkle over the spices, lemon juice and
almonds.

Bake in a preheated oven, 180°C (350°F) for
12–15 minutes.

Meanwhile, mix together the stem ginger and
yogurt in a bowl.

Serve the bananas with dollops of the yogurt.

Your body needs time to shift into sleep mode, so
it can help to spend the last hour before bed doing
something calming such as reading.

INSOMNIA

spinach & stilton salad

THE SCIENCE BIT

According to University of Texas research, walnuts contain melatonin which may help you to fall asleep faster.

SERVES 4
Prep + cook time: 10 minutes
   + cooling

1 tablespoon clear honey
125 g (4 oz) walnut halves
250 g (8 oz) French-style green
   beans, trimmed
200 g (7 oz) baby spinach leaves
150 g (5 oz) Stilton cheese,
   crumbled

walnut dressing
4 tablespoons walnut oil
2 tablespoons extra-virgin olive oil
1–2 tablespoons sherry vinegar
salt and pepper

Heat the honey in a small frying pan, add the walnuts and stir-fry over a medium heat for 2–3 minutes until the nuts are glazed. Tip on to a plate and leave to cool.

Meanwhile, cook the beans in a saucepan of lightly salted boiling water for 3 minutes. Drain, refresh under cold water and shake dry. Put in a large bowl with the spinach leaves.

Whisk all the dressing ingredients together in a small bowl and season with salt and pepper. Pour over the salad and toss well. Arrange the salad in serving bowls, scatter over the Stilton and glazed walnuts and serve immediately.

The spinach and cheese in this salad are also insomnia-beaters: they're loaded with calcium which helps the body convert tryptophan to melatonin.

toasted peanut & wild rice salad

THE SCIENCE BIT

Australian research found that people who ate rice before bedtime fell asleep faster as rice is rich in sugars, which increase production of tryptophan.

SERVES 2

Prep + cook time: 35 minutes

125 g (4 oz) basmati rice
25 g (1 oz) wild rice
1 bunch of scallions, chopped
125 g (4 oz) raisins
125 g (4 oz) toasted peanuts
4 tablespoons balsamic vinegar
1 tablespoon sunflower oil

Cook both types of rice according to the instructions on the packets. Rinse in cold water and drain thoroughly.

Mix together the cooked rice, scallions, raisins and peanuts in a large bowl.

Pour the vinegar and oil into a small bowl and whisk together, then stir the dressing into the rice mixture.

Sleep experts recommend practising "sleep hygiene" to combat insomnia, which means making sure your bedroom is clean, comfortable, dark, quiet and not too warm.

ARTHRITIS

grilled fruit parcels with pistachio yogurt

THE SCIENCE BIT

Nuts that are rich in omega-3 fatty acids, such as the pistachios in this healthy dessert recipe, can ease stiffness and reduce inflammation.

SERVES 2

Prep + cook time: 20 minutes

125 g (4 oz) mixed blueberries and
   raspberries
2 peaches or nectarines, halved,
   pitted and sliced
½ cinnamon stick, halved
1 tablespoon clear honey
2 tablespoons orange juice
25 g (1 oz) shelled pistachio nuts,
   chopped, plus extra to decorate
4 tablespoons Greek natural yogurt

Cut 2 large, double thickness squares of foil. Divide the fruit and cinnamon between the squares and drizzle over the honey and orange juice. Fold the foil over the filling and scrunch the edges to seal.

Place the parcels under a preheated medium grill or on a barbecue for about 10 minutes until the fruit is soft and hot.

Open the parcels carefully and transfer the fruit to serving bowls.

Mix together the pistachios and yogurt in a bowl. Serve with an extra sprinkling of pistachios and spoon the yogurt over the warm fruit.

Berries top the charts in antioxidant power, protecting your body against inflammation and free radicals, the molecules that can damage cells and organs.

ARTHRITIS

bean burgers with garlicky yogurt

THE SCIENCE BIT
Some research suggests that regularly consuming alpha-linolenic acid, found in kidney beans, can alleviate joint stiffness and reduce inflammation in people with arthritis.

SERVES 4
Prep + cook time: 30 minutes

3 tablespoons vegetable oil
1 onion, finely chopped
1 garlic clove, chopped
400 g (13 oz) can red kidney beans, rinsed and drained
400 g (13 oz) can black-eyed beans, rinsed and drained
1 tablespoon tomato purée
1 teaspoon paprika (optional)
4 tablespoons finely chopped flat leaf parsley
1 small egg, lightly beaten
100 g (3½ oz) fresh white breadcrumbs
250 ml (8 fl oz) natural yogurt
1 small garlic clove, crushed
2 teaspoons lemon juice
salt and pepper
4 warmed soft flour tortillas and lettuce leaves, to serve

Heat 2 tablespoons of the oil in a small frying pan and cook the onion gently for 6–7 minutes. Add the chopped garlic and cook for a further 2–3 minutes, until really soft and golden.

Meanwhile, place both lots of beans in the large bowl of a food processor with the tomato purée, paprika, if using, and half the parsley. Pulse until the mixture becomes a coarse paste. Tip into a bowl and add the egg, breadcrumbs and cooked onion mixture. Season with salt and pepper, then mix well and shape into 4 large burgers.

Heat the remaining oil in a large nonstick frying pan and fry the burgers gently for 8–10 minutes, turning once, until crisp and golden.

Meanwhile, mix the yogurt with the crushed garlic, the remaining parsley and the lemon juice. Season with salt and pepper and set aside.

Serve the burgers with warmed tortillas and the yogurt and lettuce leaves.

marinated tofu & mushroom salad

THE SCIENCE BIT

High in protein and low in fat, soya protein in tofu has also been shown to reduce pain and swelling.

SERVES 4

Prep + cook time: 20 minutes
+ marinating

250 g (8 oz) firm tofu
500 g (1 lb) mushrooms, including
enoki, shiitake, wood ear and
oyster

marinade
1 garlic clove, finely chopped
2 cm (¾ inch) fresh ginger, peeled
and finely sliced
5 tablespoons soy sauce
1 tablespoon mirin
2 tablespoons sweet chilli sauce
1½ tablespoons sesame oil
2 star anise
5 finely sliced scallions and 2
tablespoons toasted sesame
seeds, to garnish

Make the marinade. Mix the garlic and ginger with the soy sauce, mirin, sweet chilli sauce and oil. Add the star anise.

Put the tofu in a non-metallic dish, pour over the marinade, cover and refrigerate for at least 2 hours or overnight if possible.

Cut the mushrooms into bite-sized pieces and sauté in a hot saucepan for 1 minute. Cut the marinated tofu into 2 cm (¾ inch) squares, mix with the mushrooms and pour over the remaining marinade. Garnish with finely sliced scallions and sesame seeds and serve immediately.

Mushrooms are a good source of B vitamins, which help provide energy by breaking down proteins, fats and carbohydrates, and play a key role in the nervous system.

broccoli & chilli pasta

THE SCIENCE BIT

One study found that a compound in broccoli called sulforaphane may block the enzymes that cause joint destruction in osteoarthritis.

SERVES 4
Prep + cook time: 20 minutes

350 g (11½ oz) broccoli, cut into
    florets
300 g (10 oz) orecchiette pasta
4 tablespoons olive oil
3 shallots, diced
4 garlic cloves, finely chopped
1 teaspoon dried chili flakes
2 tablespoons chopped parsley
2 tablespoons Parmesan-style
    cheese shavings, to serve

Steam the broccoli for 4–5 minutes, until just tender and drain.

Cook the orecchiette in a saucepan of boiling water for 11–13 minutes, or according to packet instructions, until al dente.

Meanwhile, heat 2 tablespoons of the olive oil in a frying pan and sauté the shallots with the garlic and chili flakes for 3–4 minutes.

Add the broccoli to the frying pan and stir to coat with the spicy oil.

Drain the pasta and add to the frying pan with the remaining oil and chopped parsley. Toss together well. Serve sprinkled with cheese shavings.

One of the kindest things you can do for your body is to maintain a healthy weight, which will relieve tension in your joints, reduce pain and improve mobility.

ANAEMIA

quick parsnip & lentil dhal

THE SCIENCE BIT

The lentils in this dhal provide iron and combining these with spinach, which contains both iron and vitamin C, makes it easier for your body to absorb.

SERVES 4–6
Prep + cook time: 30 minutes

300 g (10 oz) split red lentils, rinsed
2 tablespoons vegetable oil
1 onion, finely chopped
2 garlic cloves, crushed
1 tablespoon peeled and grated fresh ginger
2 teaspoons mild curry powder
1 teaspoon garam masala
½ teaspoon ground turmeric
500 g (1 lb) parsnips, diced
400 ml (14 fl oz) hot vegetable stock (see page 9 for homemade)
2 tablespoons coconut cream
150 g (5 oz) spinach leaves, roughly chopped
salt and pepper
naan bread, to serve

Cook the lentils in a pan of boiling water for 15 minutes, or according to the packet instructions, until tender.

Meanwhile, heat the vegetable oil in a large saucepan and cook the onion, garlic and ginger for 5–6 minutes over a medium heat, stirring frequently, until starting to color. Add the spices and parsnips, cook for 1 minute, then add the stock and coconut cream and cook for about 10 minutes, until tender.

Drain the lentils and add to the stock pan. Add the spinach and stir for 1 minute, until wilted. Season to taste, then spoon into bowls and serve with naan bread.

Iron deficiency is the leading cause of anaemia, when the body has a lower-than-normal red blood cell count.

ANAEMIA

peach, feta & watercress salad

THE SCIENCE BIT

In addition to being a good source of plant-based iron, peppery watercress contains vitamins A, B6, B12, magnesium, calcium and phosphorus.

SERVES 4
Prep + cook time: 10 minutes

30 g (1 oz) pumpkin seeds
juice of ½ lemon
2 tablespoons extra-virgin olive oil
½ teaspoon Dijon mustard
1 teaspoon honey
1 tablespoon chopped oregano
75 g (3 oz) watercress
3 peaches, halved, pitted and sliced
4 scallions, sliced
175 g (6 oz) feta cheese, crumbled
pepper

Heat a nonstick frying pan over a medium-low heat and dry-fry the pumpkin seeds for 2–3 minutes, stirring frequently, until slightly golden and toasted. Set aside.

Whisk together the lemon juice, oil, mustard, honey, oregano and pepper in a small bowl.

Divide the watercress among 4 plates, top with the peach slices and scallions, then sprinkle over the feta cheese.

Serve sprinkled with the toasted pumpkin seeds and drizzled with the dressing.

Who doesn't love a juicy peach? Peaches are full of vitamins A, C, E and K, as well as providing iron.

ANAEMIA

asparagus frittata

THE SCIENCE BIT

The eggs in this delicious frittata are an excellent vegetarian source of haeme iron, and the asparagus contains vitamins A, C, E and K.

SERVES 4
Prep + cook time: 30 minutes

400 g (13 oz) asparagus
2 tablespoons olive oil
6 large eggs
50 g (2 oz) Parmesan-style cheese, grated
1 tablespoon chopped oregano
salt and pepper

Break the woody ends off the asparagus and discard. Toss the spears in 1 tablespoon of the olive oil.

Heat a griddle pan until hot and cook the asparagus for 4–5 minutes, until starting to look a little charred. Cut the asparagus spears into thirds.

Beat the eggs in a large bowl with the grated cheese, oregano and some salt and pepper. Add the asparagus.

Heat the remaining oil in a flameproof, nonstick frying pan. Pour the mixture into the pan and cook for 8–10 minutes over a low heat, tipping the pan from time to time to allow the runny egg to reach the edges to cook evenly.

Cook for a further 4–5 minutes under a preheated hot grill, until the top is golden.

Turn the frittata out on to a board, cut into wedges and serve immediately.

ANAEMIA

poached apricots with pistachios

THE SCIENCE BIT

Foods that are high in iron, such as dried apricots, fight the tiredness and lethargy caused by iron-deficient anaemia.

SERVES 4

Prep + cook time: 10 minutes

400 g (13 oz) ready-to-eat
    semi-dried apricots
350 ml (12 fl oz) apple and
    elderflower juice
2 tablespoons orange flower water
½ teaspoon ground cinnamon
2 tablespoons clear honey
75 g (3 oz) shelled unsalted
    pistachios, crushed

Put the apricots in a pan with the apple and elderflower juice, orange flower water, cinnamon and honey and bring to a gentle boil over a medium-high heat. Reduce the heat and simmer for 2–3 minutes until fragrant.

Pour the apricots and juices into a large bowl and set aside to cool slightly.

Serve in deep bowls, scattered with the pistachios.

Made from orange blossoms, orange flower water – also called orange blossom water – is a clear liquid with an strong floral-orange aroma. When using it in a recipe, start by adding a small amount as the scent is intense.

BLOOD PRESSURE

breakfast smoothie

THE SCIENCE BIT

Kick-start your day with this super-healthy smoothie which has banana to provide potassium plus high-fiber, low-fat, low-sodium oats.

SERVES 2–3
Prep time: 10 minutes

1 tablespoon pomegranate juice
1 small banana, chopped
300 ml (½ pint) soy milk
1 tablespoon almonds
1 tablespoon rolled oats
½ teaspoon honey
½ tablespoon ground linseeds
2 tablespoons natural yogurt

Place all the ingredients in a blender or food processor and blend until smooth and creamy.

Pour into 2 glasses and serve immediately.

One study showed that drinking pomegranate juice every day can help to lower blood pressure naturally. Keep it healthy by making sure it has no added sugar, though.

butternut, kale & mixed bean soup

THE SCIENCE BIT

Kale is a major source of vitamin K, to ward off heart disease, and fiber to lower blood pressure.

SERVES 6
Prep + cook time: 1 hour

1 tablespoon olive oil
1 onion, finely chopped
2 garlic cloves, finely chopped
1 teaspoon smoked paprika
500 g (1 lb) butternut squash, halved, deseeded, peeled and diced
2 small carrots, diced
500 g (1 lb) tomatoes, skinned (optional) and roughly chopped
400 g (13 oz) can mixed beans, rinsed and drained
900 ml (1½ pints) vegetable stock (see page 9 for homemade)
150 ml (¼ pint) crème fraîche
100 g (3½ oz) kale, torn into bite-sized pieces
pepper
garlic bread, to serve (optional)

Heat the oil in a saucepan over a medium-low heat, add the onion and fry gently for 5 minutes. Stir in the garlic and smoked paprika and cook briefly, then add the squash, carrots, tomatoes and mixed beans.

Pour in the stock, season with salt and pepper and bring to the boil, stirring frequently. Reduce the heat, cover and simmer for 25 minutes or until the vegetables are tender.

Stir in the crème fraîche, then add the kale, pressing it just beneath the surface of the stock. Cover and cook for 5 minutes or until the kale has just wilted. Ladle into bowls and serve with warm garlic bread, if liked.

Aside from providing vegetarians with essential protein, beans contain magnesium which aids nerve function and blood pressure regulation.

roasted carrot & red beets pearl barley with feta

THE SCIENCE BIT

Potassium in vegetables like red beets and carrots helps balance out the negative effects of salt which has a direct effect on lowering blood pressure.

SERVES 4

Prep + cook time: 40 minutes

2 red onions, cut into slim wedges

16 bunched carrots, scrubbed and cut into chunks

1 large raw red beets, about 300 g (10 oz), peeled and cut into slim wedges

olive oil

1½ teaspoons cumin seeds

1½ teaspoons ground cilantro

1½ vegetable stock cubes

275 g (9 oz) pearl barley

300 g (10 oz) feta cheese, crumbled

6 tablespoons cilantro leaves

Place all the prepared vegetables in a large roasting tin, drizzle with the oil and toss to coat. Add the cumin seeds and ground cilantro and toss again. Place at the top of a preheated oven, 220°C (425°F) for 20–25 minutes until the vegetables are tender and lightly charred in places.

Meanwhile, bring a large saucepan of water to the boil, add the stock cubes and pearl barley and cook for 20 minutes until the grain is tender. Drain, then toss with the vegetables.

Add the crumbled feta and cilantro leaves, toss well and serve.

Take care when preparing red beets as the bright juice can stain hands and clothing.

spinach & potato tortilla

THE SCIENCE BIT

Among many other health benefits, the potatoes and spinach in this tortilla are high in potassium for better blood pressure.

SERVES 4
Prep + cook time: 30 minutes

3 tablespoons olive oil
2 onions, finely chopped
250 g (8 oz) cooked potatoes,
  peeled and cut into 1 cm
  (½ in) cubes
2 garlic cloves, finely chopped
200 g (7 oz) cooked spinach,
  drained thoroughly and
  roughly chopped
4 tablespoons finely chopped
  roasted red pepper
5 eggs, lightly beaten
3–4 tablespoons grated vegetarian
  Manchego cheese
pepper

Heat the oil in a nonstick frying pan and add the onions and potatoes. Cook gently over a medium heat for 3–4 minutes or until the vegetables have softened but not colored, turning and stirring often. Add the garlic, spinach and peppers and stir to mix well.

Beat the eggs lightly and season well with pepper. Pour into the frying pan, shaking the pan so that the egg is evenly spread.

Cook gently for 8–10 minutes or until the tortilla is set at the bottom.

Sprinkle over the grated Manchego. Place the frying pan under a preheated medium-hot grill and cook for 3–4 minutes or until the top is set and golden brown.

Remove from the heat, cut the tortilla into bite-sized squares or triangles and serve warm or at room temperature.

STOMACH SOOTHERS

quick & easy miso soup

THE SCIENCE BIT

Miso is a fermented paste
that it is packed with probiotics,
the bacteria that help promote
a healthy gut.

SERVES 4
Prep + cook time: 20 minutes

1.8 litres (3 pints) vegetable stock
   (see page 9 for homemade)
2 tablespoons miso paste
125 g (4 oz) shiitake mushrooms,
   sliced
200 g (7 oz) firm tofu, cubed
cooked rice, to serve

Put the stock in a saucepan and heat until simmering.

Add the miso paste, shiitake mushrooms and tofu to the stock and simmer gently for 5 minutes. Serve immediately with rice.

Tummy in a knot? Stand still with your eyes closed and breathe slowly as you relax one part of your body at a time to release tension throughout your body, including your stomach.

cumin lentils with yogurt dressing

THE SCIENCE BIT

Probiotics in Greek yogurt aid in digestion and reduce the uncomfortable feeling of being bloated.

SERVES 4
Prep + cook time: 25 minutes
  + cooling

4 tablespoons olive oil
2 red onions, thinly sliced
2 garlic cloves, chopped
2 teaspoon cumin seeds
500 g (1 lb) cooked Puy lentils
125 g (4 oz) peppery leaves, such as
  red beets or arugula
1 large raw red beet, peeled and
  coarsely grated
1 Granny Smith apple, peeled and
  coarsely grated (optional)
lemon juice, to serve
salt and pepper

yogurt dressing
300 ml (½ pint) Greek yogurt
2 tablespoons lemon juice
½ teaspoon ground cumin
15 g (½ oz) mint leaves, chopped

Heat the oil in a frying pan and fry the red onions over a medium heat for about 8 minutes until soft and golden. Add the garlic and cumin seeds and cook for a further 5 minutes.

Mix the onion mixture into the lentils, season well and leave to cool.

Make the dressing by mixing together the ingredients in a small bowl.

Serve the cooled lentils on a bed of leaves, with the grated red beet and apple, if using, a couple of spoonfuls of minty yogurt and a generous squeeze of lemon juice.

Grown in the Le Puy region of France, dark green Puy lentils have a peppery taste and hold their shape well during cooking.

breakfast banana split

THE SCIENCE BIT

Easy-to-digest banana is a natural tummy soother and honey helps to coat the stomach lining.

SERVES 4
Prep + cook time: 10 minutes

50 g (2 oz) unsalted butter
2 tablespoons clear honey
4 bananas, cut in half lengthways
2 dessert apples, grated
300 g (10 oz) Greek yogurt
finely grated rind of 1 orange
50 g (2 oz) walnuts, toasted
2 tablespoons flaked almonds,
  toasted
2–3 tablespoons maple syrup

Melt the butter in a frying pan with the honey until it sizzles.

Place the bananas in the frying pan, cut side down, and cook for 3–4 minutes, until golden.

Meanwhile, mix together the grated apple, yogurt and orange rind.

Transfer the bananas onto 4 plates and top with a large dollop of the yogurt mixture.

Sprinkle over the nuts, then drizzle with the maple syrup and any juices from the pan to serve.

Research has shown that regular consumption of small amounts of nuts, such as the walnuts in this banana split, can reduce the risk of heart disease, some types of cancer, type two diabetes and other health problems.

HEARTBURN

Mediterranean rice salad

THE SCIENCE BIT

Recipes that contain naturally low-acid food like rice are a good choice if you have acid reflux.

SERVES 4

Prep + cook time: 15 minutes
  + cooling

75 g (3 oz) broccoli, finely chopped
75 g (3 oz) zucchinis, finely chopped
75 g (3 oz) mixed red and yellow
  peppers, cored, deseeded and
  finely chopped
25 g (1 oz) scallions, finely chopped
40 g (1½ oz) mushrooms, finely
  sliced
2 tablespoons water
2 tablespoons fresh green pesto
50 g (2 oz) cooked brown rice
50 g (2 oz) cooked wild rice
salt and pepper
Parmesan-style cheese and basil
  leaves, to serve (optional)

Heat a large frying pan or wok, add the vegetables and the measurement water and cook over a high heat for 3–5 minutes, until the vegetables have softened. Remove from the heat and allow to cool.

Mix the cooled vegetables with the pesto and cooked rice, season well and stir to combine. Serve topped with a few cheese shavings and some basil leaves, if liked.

To help heartburn try eating smaller, more frequent meals throughout the day, and be sure to chew food completely.

HEARTBURN

cauliflower & cumin soup

THE SCIENCE BIT

Take it slow – feeling stressed or eating on the go can cause the stomach to produce more acids and increase the likelihood of heartburn.

SERVES 4
Prep + cook time: 25 minutes

2 teaspoons sunflower oil
1 onion, chopped
1 garlic clove, crushed
2 teaspoons cumin seeds
1 cauliflower, cut into florets
1 large potato, peeled and chopped
450 ml (¾ pint) vegetable stock
    (see page 9 for homemade)
450 ml (¾ pint) milk
2 tablespoons crème fraîche
2 tablespoons chopped cilantro
    leaves
salt and pepper
crusty wholemeal bread, to serve

Heat the oil in a medium saucepan and fry the onion, garlic and cumin seeds for 3–4 minutes. Add the cauliflower, potato, stock and milk and bring to the boil. Reduce the heat and simmer for 15 minutes.

Blend the soup until smooth. Stir through the crème fraîche and cilantro and season to taste with salt and pepper. Heat through and serve with slices of crusty wholemeal bread.

The cauliflower in this creamy soup is low in acid. Broccoli and green beans are other low-acid vegetable options.

HEARTBURN

bulgur wheat, goats' cheese & red onion

THE SCIENCE BIT

Complex carbohydrates like bulgur wheat can help soothe your stomach and prevent acid travelling back up into the oesophagus.

SERVES 4

Prep + cook time: 20 minutes

750 ml (1¼ pints) hot vegetable stock (see page 9 for homemade)

275 g (9 oz) bulgur wheat

4 tablespoons olive or vegetable oil

1 large red onion, halved and thinly sliced

100 ml (3½ fl oz) tomato juice

2 tablespoons lime juice

175 g (6 oz) firm goats' cheese, crumbled

3 tablespoons roughly chopped flat leaf parsley

salt and pepper

Bring the vegetable stock to the boil in a large saucepan, add the bulgur wheat and cook for 7 minutes. Remove from the heat, cover with a tight-fitting lid and set aside for 5–8 minutes, until the liquid has been absorbed and the grains are tender.

Meanwhile, heat 2 tablespoons of oil in a frying pan and cook the onion gently for 7–8 minutes, until soft and golden.

Combine the remaining oil with the tomato juice and lime juice, and season with salt and pepper. Fold the dressing, onion, goats' cheese and parsley into the bulgur wheat with a fork, and spoon into 4 shallow bowls to serve.

Parsley adds a fresh taste to this salad and there is some evidence that it can help ease heartburn too.

VEGETARIAN RECIPES FOR SOUL AND SPIRIT

introduction

We all know that the better your diet, the better your physical health. But what you eat can influence brain chemistry and affect your emotional health and mood too. Eating a well-balanced vegetarian diet, along with regular exercise, will help to banish the blues and make you feel happier.

Sleep also plays a vital role in good health and wellbeing throughout your life. Getting enough sleep will help protect both mental and physical wellbeing, and improve your quality of life on a daily basis.

The feel-good recipes in this chapter offer something for every occasion, make the best of seasonal produce, grains and protein, and even include that favorite mood-booster, chocolate.

purple broccoli linguine with poached eggs

THE SCIENCE BIT

The tryptophan in eggs converts to serotonin, the neurotransmitter that is responsible for mood balance.

SERVES 4

Prep + cook time: 20 minutes

300 g (10 oz) linguine
250 g (8 oz) purple sprouting broccoli
4 eggs
2 tablespoons olive oil
6 scallions, sliced
1 teaspoon dried chili flakes
12 cherry tomatoes, halved

Cook the pasta in a large saucepan of boiling water for 6 minutes. Add the broccoli and cook for a further 4–5 minutes until the pasta is "al dente" and the broccoli is tender.

Meanwhile, bring a saucepan of water to a gentle simmer and stir with a large spoon to create a swirl. Break 2 of the eggs into the water and cook for 3 minutes. Remove with a slotted spoon and keep warm. Repeat with the remaining eggs.

Drain the pasta and broccoli and keep warm. Heat the oil in the pasta pan, add the scallions, chili flakes and tomatoes and fry, stirring, for 2–3 minutes. Return the pasta and broccoli to the pan and toss well to coat with the chilli oil.

Serve the pasta topped with the poached eggs.

Put your hands to work to help your mind unwind. Hobbies like knitting, sewing and woodwork can help relieve stress.

spiced potato, cilantro & celeriac soup

THE SCIENCE BIT

Studies show that the scent of lavender can lower blood pressure and heart rate and change brain waves to a more relaxed state.

SERVES 4
Prep + cook time: 30 minutes

1 onion, chopped
2 tablespoons olive oil
1 garlic clove, chopped
½ teaspoons each of ground cumin and cilantro
pinch of chili flakes
2 small celeriac, peeled and finely diced
2 medium potatoes, peeled and finely diced
1 litre (1¾ pint) hot vegetable stock (see page 9 for homemade)
25 g (1 oz) chopped cilantro
4 tablespoons crème fraîche, to serve
toasted cumin seeds, to garnish

Place the onion and olive oil in a pan with the garlic, ground cumin and cilantro and a pinch of chili flakes. Fry over a medium heat for 1 minute.

Add the celeriac and potato, cover with the hot vegetable stock and bring to the boil. Simmer for 15–20 minutes or until the vegetables are tender.

Stir in the chopped cilantro and blend until fairly smooth.

Ladle into bowls and serve with a dollop of crème fraîche and toasted cumin seeds.

An American research team found that the body loses its ability to fight off infections when it's constantly under stress which is why garlic is such a great ingredient in many dishes, like this soup – it's been shown to combat stress and fatigue.

cheesy baked leeks & sweet potatoes

THE SCIENCE BIT

Sweet potatoes contain beta-carotene, to increase immunity when stress levels are soaring, and tryptophan which converts to feel-good serotonin.

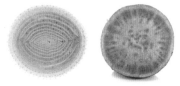

SERVES 4
Prep + cook time: 40 minutes

4 small sweet potatoes
4 teaspoons sea salt
4 leeks, trimmed, halved and sliced
150 ml (¼ pint) white wine
2 tablespoons extra-virgin olive oil
75 g (3 oz) Parmesan-style cheese, grated
2 garlic cloves, crushed
40 g (1¾ oz) pine nuts
pepper

Prick the sweet potatoes with a knife or fork, then wash and rub with the salt. Bake in a preheated oven, 200°C (400°F) for 25 minutes until tender.

Meanwhile, place the leeks in a shallow ovenproof dish and sprinkle with the wine and oil. Season with pepper. Mix together the cheese, garlic and pine nuts in a bowl, then sprinkle over the leeks.

Cover with foil and place in the oven for 15 minutes, then remove the foil and cook for a further 12–13 minutes.

Halve the sweet potatoes and serve with the leeks.

Stress can accelerate ageing, so why not give soothing yoga or meditation a try? Meditating stimulates the pituitary gland in the brain to release endorphins, promoting relaxation and overall wellbeing.

roasted veg couscous with cashews & feta

THE SCIENCE BIT

Cashew nuts are an especially rich source of zinc which works to calm an anxious mind.

SERVES 4
Prep + cook time: 30 minutes

2 red peppers, cored, deseeded and cut into 2 cm (¾ inch) pieces
1 yellow pepper, cored, deseeded and cut into 2 cm (¾ inch) pieces
1 zucchini, cut into 2 cm (¾ inch) cubes
2 large red onions, thickly sliced
4 tablespoons olive oil
200 g (7 oz) couscous
100 g (3½ oz) cashew nuts
handful of chopped mint
handful of chopped cilantro
6–8 preserved lemons, halved
200 g (7 oz) feta cheese, crumbled
salt and pepper

orange dressing
juice of 1 orange
5 tablespoons extra-virgin olive oil
1 red chilli, finely chopped
1 teaspoon each smoked paprika, ground cumin, mild curry powder

Put the vegetables on a large baking sheet, drizzle with the oil and season well. Place in a preheated oven, 200°C (400°F) for 12–15 minutes until softened and just starting to char at the edges.

Meanwhile, put the couscous in a large heatproof bowl and season well. Pour over boiling water to just cover, then cover with clingfilm and leave to stand for 8–10 minutes, or according to the packet instructions, until the water is absorbed.

Make the dressing: mix together all the ingredients in a bowl and season well, then set aside.

Toast the cashews: heat a frying pan until hot, add the cashews and dry-fry over a medium heat until light brown. Remove from the pan and set aside.

Gently fork the couscous to separate the grains. Place in a large serving dish and fold in the vegetables, herbs and preserved lemons. Pour over the dressing and toss to mix well. Scatter with the toasted cashews and feta cheese and serve.

DEPRESSION

porridge with prune compote

THE SCIENCE BIT

Porridge is the ultimate feel-good breakfast: oats contain tryptophan to raise your mood and milk has potassium to relax tense muscles.

SERVES 4–8

Prep + cook time: 25 minutes
  + cooling

1 litre (1¾ pints) milk
500 ml (17 fl oz) water
1 teaspoon vanilla extract
pinch of ground cinnamon
pinch of salt
200 g (7 oz) porridge oats
3 tablespoons flaked almonds,
  toasted

compote
250 g (8 oz) ready-to-eat dried
  Agen prunes
125 ml (4 fl oz) apple juice
1 small cinnamon stick
1 clove
1 tablespoon mild agave nectar or
  runny honey
1 unpeeled orange quarter

Place all the compote ingredients in a small saucepan over a medium heat. Simmer gently for 10–12 minutes or until softened and slightly sticky. Leave to cool. (The compote can be prepared in advance and chilled.)

Put the milk, measurement water, vanilla extract, cinnamon and salt in a large saucepan over a medium heat and bring slowly to the boil. Stir in the oats, then reduce the heat and simmer gently, stirring occasionally, for 8–10 minutes until creamy and tender.

Spoon the porridge into bowls, scatter with the almonds and serve with the prune compote.

Prunes are high in fiber and also contain iron, potassium and boron which helps to build strong bones and muscles.

DEPRESSION

spiced fruit salad

THE SCIENCE BIT

Research suggest that the flavonoids found in blueberries help "happy" dopamine neurons in the brain survive much longer.

SERVES 6

Prep + cook time: 15 minutes
  + cooling and chilling

1 vanilla pod, plus extra for
  decorating, if liked
2½ tablespoons superfine sugar
175 ml (6 fl oz) water
1 hot red chilli
4 clementines
2 peaches
½ cantaloupe melon
175 g (6 oz) blueberries

Use the tip of a small, sharp knife to score the vanilla pod lengthways through to the center. Put the sugar and water in a saucepan and heat gently until the sugar dissolves. Halve and deseed the chilli and add it to the saucepan with the vanilla pod. Heat gently for 2 minutes, then remove the pan from the heat and leave the syrup to cool.

Cut away the rind from the clementines and slice the flesh. Remove the pits from the peaches and slice the flesh. Deseed the melon and cut the flesh into small chunks, discarding the skin.

Mix the fruits in a serving dish and pour over the warm syrup, discarding the chilli and vanilla pod. Leave the syrup to cool completely, then cover the fruit salad and chill until you are ready to serve. Decorate with a vanilla pod if liked.

Studies by Stanford University in the USA found that participants who spent 50 minutes walking in a city park experienced a boost in mood as well as in their working memories and attention.

DEPRESSION

asparagus & pea quinoa risotto

THE SCIENCE BIT

Eat mood-enhancing asparagus to provide plenty of folic acid, low levels of which have been linked to depression.

SERVES 4
Prep + cook time: 20 minutes

275 g (9 oz) quinoa, rinsed
600 ml (1 pint) hot vegetable stock
   (see page 9 for homemade)
200 g (7 oz) asparagus, chopped
200 g (7 oz) frozen peas
1 tablespoon chopped mint
3 tablespoons grated Parmesan-style
   cheese
pepper

Place the quinoa and stock in a saucepan and bring to the boil, then reduce the heat and simmer for 12–15 minutes until the quinoa is cooked, adding the asparagus and peas about 2 minutes before the end of the cooking time.

Drain the quinoa and vegetables, then return to the pan with the mint and 2 tablespoons of the cheese and season with pepper. Mix well.

Serve sprinkled with the remaining cheese.

When you smile, even if you don't feel happy, it compresses the blood vessels in your face sending more blood to the brain and triggering a genuine feeling of happiness.

DEPRESSION

roasted red pepper & walnut dip

THE SCIENCE BIT

Rich in omega-3 fatty acids, studies suggest that walnuts can help support brain function and reduce symptoms of depression.

SERVES 4–6

Prep + cook time: 20 minutes
  + cooling

4 large red peppers
75 g (3 oz) walnut pieces
juice of 1 lemon
1 tablespoon pomegranate molasses
½ teaspoon chilli paste
1 tablespoon olive oil
salt and pepper
pomegranate seeds, mint leaves and
  flatbreads (optional), to serve

Cut each pepper into quarters and remove and discard the core and seeds. Place skin-side up under a preheated high grill and cook until the skin is blackened. Transfer to a food bag and leave until cool enough to handle.

Remove and discard the blackened skins from the peppers and place the pepper flesh on kitchen paper to remove the excess moisture.

Place the walnuts in a food processor and process until finely ground. Add all the remaining ingredients, then process until smooth.

Scrape the mixture into a bowl and season to taste with salt and pepper. Serve garnished with pomegranate seeds and mint leaves, with warmed flatbreads, if liked.

Pomegranate molasses is a traditional Middle Eastern ingredient and is a treacly syrup with a sweet, yet sharp, flavor.

EMOTIONAL WELLBEING

gazpacho

THE SCIENCE BIT

Packed with antioxidants,
a daily dose of garlic in your
meals will benefit your
immune system.

SERVES 4
Prep + cook time: 20 minutes

4 red peppers, cored, deseeded and
   roughly chopped
1 red onion, roughly chopped
2 cucumbers, roughly chopped
handful of basil leaves
handful of parsley leaves
2 garlic cloves
2 tablespoons sherry vinegar or
   balsamic vinegar
150 ml (¼ pint) olive oil
450 ml (¾ pint) chilled tomato juice
salt and pepper

to serve
1 avocado, peeled, pitted and
   chopped
1 soft-boiled egg, quartered

Place the vegetables, herbs and garlic in the food
processor and process until finely chopped.

Add the remaining ingredients, season to taste and
process again briefly. Cover and chill for 5 minutes.

Serve in bowls topped with the chopped avocados
and quartered eggs.

Chilled soups like this Spanish classic are a great
addition to the outdoor dining table. Enjoy it as light
supper or lunch or serve in small portions as a pre-
barbecue starter.

warm chocolate fromage frais

THE SCIENCE BIT

Dark chocolate stimulates the production of endorphins, chemicals in our brains that bring on feelings of pleasure.

SERVES 6
Prep + cook time: 5 minutes

300 g (10 oz) plain dark chocolate
500 g (1 lb) fromage frais
1 teaspoon vanilla extract

Melt the chocolate in a bowl over a pan of simmering water, then remove from the heat.

Add the fromage frais and vanilla extract and quickly stir together.

Divide the chocolate fromage frais among 6 small pots or glasses and serve immediately.

Dark chocolate helps protect heart health, regulate blood pressure, reduce risk of heart attack and help prevent age-related dementia.

EMOTIONAL WELLBEING

red beets & squash spaghetti

THE SCIENCE BIT

You can improve emotional balance by improving your nutritional balance, so include healthy fats, complex carbohydrates and protein in your daily diet.

SERVES 4
Prep + cook time: 20 minutes

300 g (10 oz) dried spaghetti or
   fusilli
150 g (5 oz) fine green beans
500 g (1 lb) butternut squash,
   peeled, deseeded and cut into
   1 cm (½ inch) dice
4 tablespoons olive oil
500 g (1 lb) raw red beets, cut into
   1 cm (½ inch) dice
50 g (2 oz) walnuts, crushed
150 g (5 oz) goats' cheese, diced
2 tablespoons lemon juice
freshly grated Parmesan-style
   cheese, to serve (optional)

Cook the pasta in lightly salted boiling water for 10 minutes or until just cooked. Add the beans and squash for the final 2 minutes of cooking time.

Meanwhile, heat the oil in a large frying pan, add the red beets and cook, stirring occasionally, for 10 minutes until cooked but still firm.

Toss the drained pasta mixture with the red beets, walnuts and goats' cheese. Squeeze over the lemon juice and serve immediately with a bowl of cheese, if liked.

Butternut squash provides significant amounts of potassium, important for bone health, and vitamin B6, essential for the proper functioning of both the nervous and immune systems.

saffron-scented vegetable tagine

THE SCIENCE BIT

Dubbed the "green-space effect", spending time outside is scientifically proven to boost your emotional wellbeing.

SERVES 4

Prep + cook time: 1 hour

100 ml (3½ fl oz) sunflower oil

1 large onion, finely chopped

2 garlic cloves, finely chopped

2 teaspoons ground cilantro

2 teaspoons ground cumin

2 teaspoons ground cinnamon

400 g (13 oz) can chickpeas, rinsed and drained

400 g (13 oz) can chopped tomatoes

600 ml (1 pint) vegetable stock (see page 9 for homemade)

¼ teaspoon saffron threads

1 large eggplant, chopped

250 g (8 oz) button mushrooms, halved if large

100 g (3½ oz) dried figs, chopped

2 tablespoons chopped cilantro

salt and pepper

steamed wholewheat couscous, to serve

Heat 2 tablespoons of the oil in a frying pan over a medium heat, add the onion, garlic and spices and cook, stirring frequently, for 5 minutes or until golden. Using a slotted spoon, transfer to a saucepan and add the chickpeas, tomatoes, stock and saffron. Season with salt and pepper.

Heat the remaining oil in the frying pan over a high heat, add the eggplant and cook, stirring frequently, for 5 minutes or until browned. Add to the stew and bring to the boil, then reduce the heat, cover and simmer gently for 20 minutes.

Stir in the mushrooms and figs and simmer gently, uncovered, for a further 20 minutes. Stir in the chopped cilantro and season to taste. Serve with steamed wholewheat couscous.

Researchers from University College, London, discovered that Mediterranean-style eaters, who ate a diet full of vegetables and legumes, were 30 per cent less likely to develop depression.

ginger rice noodles

THE SCIENCE BIT

According to Ayurvedic medicine, ginger can help break down the accumulation of toxins in your organs.

SERVES 4
Prep + cook time: 15 minutes

100 g (3½ oz) fine rice noodles
125 g (4 oz) green beans, halved
finely grated rind and juice of
   2 limes
1 Thai chilli, deseeded and finely
   chopped
2.5 cm (1 inch) piece of fresh ginger,
   peeled and finely chopped
2 teaspoons superfine sugar
small handful of cilantro leaves,
   chopped
50 g (2 oz) dried pineapple pieces,
   chopped

Place the noodles in a bowl, cover with plenty of boiling water and leave for 4 minutes until soft.

Meanwhile, cook the beans in boiling water for about 3 minutes until tender. Drain.

Mix together the lime rind and juice, chilli, ginger, superfine sugar and cilantro in a small bowl.

Drain the noodles and place in a large serving bowl. Add the cooked beans, pineapple and dressing and toss together lightly before serving.

The chilli in this recipe does more than just add spice. Researchers found that the compounds that give chillies their heat can lower high blood pressure and reduce blood cholesterol.

SPRING RENEWAL

spring vegetable salad

THE SCIENCE BIT

Because they have relatively high protein levels, the peas in this salad have a "feeling full" factor that will stop you reaching for snacks.

SERVES 4
Prep + cook time: 20 minutes

200 g (7 oz) fresh or frozen peas
200 g (7 oz) asparagus, trimmed
200 g (7 oz) sugar snap peas
2 zucchinis
1 fennel bulb

honey dressing
grated rind and juice of 1 lemon
1 teaspoon Dijon mustard
1 teaspoon clear honey
1 tablespoon chopped flat leaf
  parsley
1 tablespoon olive oil

Put the peas, asparagus and sugar snap peas in a saucepan of salted boiling water and simmer for 3 minutes. Drain, then refresh under cold running water.

Cut the zucchinis into long, thin ribbons and thinly slice the fennel. Transfer all the vegetables to a large salad bowl and mix together.

Make the dressing by whisking together the lemon rind and juice, mustard, honey, parsley and oil in another bowl. Toss the dressing through the vegetables and serve.

This is the time of year for spring cleaning. Don't forget your collection of dried herbs and spices – go through them and chuck out the old ones that have lost their aroma.

spring vegetable & herb pilaf

THE SCIENCE BIT

Green beans are an excellent source of dietary fiber plus they provide vitamins A, C and K.

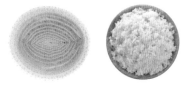

SERVES 4
Prep + cook time: 35 minutes

2 tablespoons extra-virgin olive oil
1 leek, trimmed, cleaned and sliced
1 zucchini, diced
grated rind and juice of 1 lemon
2 garlic cloves, crushed
300 g (10 oz) white long-grain rice
600 ml (1 pint) hot vegetable stock
  (see page 9 for homemade)
150 g (5 oz) green beans, chopped
150 g (5 oz) fresh or frozen peas
4 tablespoons chopped mixed herbs,
  such as mint, parsley and chives
50 g (2 oz) flaked almonds, toasted
salt and pepper

Heat the olive oil in a large frying pan, add the leek, zucchini, lemon rind, garlic and a little salt and pepper and cook gently for 5 minutes.

Add the rice, stir once and pour in the hot stock. Bring to the boil, then reduce the heat, cover and simmer gently for 10 minutes.

Stir in the beans and peas, cover and cook for a further 5 minutes.

Remove the pan from the heat and leave to stand for 5 minutes. Stir in the lemon juice and herbs and serve scattered with the flaked almonds.

The almonds that top this pilaf are rich in manganese, omega-3 fatty acids and vitamin E. Vitamin E is an antioxidant that protects the body from damage.

arugula pesto with wholewheat spaghetti

THE SCIENCE BIT

Crunchy seeds are high in protein and low in carbohydrates. Toasting them will enhance their natural flavors.

SERVES 4

Prep + cook time: 20 minutes

50 g (2 oz) sunflower or pumpkin seeds
500 g (1 lb) wholewheat spaghetti
1 small garlic clove, roughly chopped
1 small bunch of basil
75 g (3 oz) arugula leaves
25 g (1 oz) Parmesan-style cheese, finely grated, plus extra to serve (optional)
6 tablespoons olive oil
1 tablespoon lemon juice
coarse sea salt and pepper

Place the seeds in a small, dry frying pan and toast gently for 3–4 minutes, shaking the pan frequently, until lightly toasted and golden. Tip on to a plate to cool.

Cook the spaghetti in a large saucepan of lightly salted boiling water for 11–12 minutes, or according to packet instructions, until al dente.

Meanwhile, crush the garlic together with a generous pinch of sea salt using a pestle and mortar. Add the basil and arugula leaves, and pound until crushed to a coarse paste.

Add the toasted seeds and pound to a paste, then transfer to a bowl and stir in the cheese, olive oil and lemon juice. Season to taste with plenty of pepper and more salt, if necessary.

Drain the pasta and toss immediately with the pesto. Divide among 4 shallow bowls and serve with extra cheese, if liked.

quails' egg salad with baby spinach leaves

THE SCIENCE BIT

Popeye was right: Swedish researchers have found that spinach really does boost muscle power, by making them work more efficiently.

SERVES 4

Prep + cook time: 20 minutes

100 g (3½ oz) baby spinach

1 red onion, sliced

200 g (7 oz) yellow and red cherry
  tomatoes, halved

1 tablespoon wholegrain mustard

6 tablespoons avocado oil

juice of 1 lemon

1 teaspoon clear honey

12 quails' eggs, hard-boiled and
  shelled

salt and pepper

Place the spinach, red onion and tomatoes in a wide mixing bowl.

In another bowl, mix together the mustard, oil, lemon juice and honey. Season well and stir until well combined.

Divide the salad among 4 serving plates.

Halve 4 of the eggs, leaving the rest whole, and scatter over the salad, drizzling the dressing over each serving.

Because they are so small, quails' eggs cook very quickly. Bring a large saucepan of water to the boil and gently lower the eggs in with a spoon. Allow about 2 minutes for soft-boiled and 4 minutes for hard-boiled.

SUMMER COOLERS

haloumi with pomegranate salsa

THE SCIENCE BIT

Pomegranate seeds pack a powerful nutritional punch – they're loaded with fiber, vitamin C, vitamin K and potassium.

SERVES 4

Prep + cook time: 15 minutes

500 g (1 lb) haloumi cheese, sliced
1 tablespoon clear honey

pomegranate salsa

½ pomegranate
4 tablespoons extra-virgin olive oil
2 tablespoons chopped parsley
1 tablespoon lemon juice
1 small red chilli, deseeded and finely
  chopped
1 small garlic clove, crushed
1 teaspoon pomegranate molasses
  (optional)
salt and pepper

First make the pomegranate salsa. Carefully scoop the pomegranate seeds into a bowl, discarding all the white membrane. Stir in the remaining ingredients and season with salt and pepper.

Heat a large nonstick frying pan for 2–3 minutes until hot. Add the haloumi slices, in batches, and cook over a high heat for about 60 seconds on each side until browned and softened.

Meanwhile, warm the honey in a small saucepan until runny.

Transfer the pan-fried haloumi to serving plates and spoon over the salsa. Drizzle the honey over the haloumi and salsa, and serve immediately.

Lightening up your diet in warm weather is easy as there is a great array of wonderful healthy fruit and vegetables to make vibrant salads and stir-fries.

zucchini & herb risotto

THE SCIENCE BIT

Zucchinis contain very few calories and have a high water content, which makes them a good dieter's choice.

SERVES 4

Prep + cook time: 30 minutes

4 tablespoons butter

2 tablespoons olive oil

1 large onion, finely chopped

2 garlic cloves, finely chopped

350 g (11½ oz) risotto rice

200 ml (7 fl oz) white wine

1.5 litres (2½ pints) vegetable stock, heated to simmering (see page 9 for homemade)

200 g (7 oz) baby leaf spinach, chopped

100 g (3½ oz) zucchinis, finely diced

50 g (2 oz) Parmesan-style cheese, finely grated

1 small handful of dill, mint and chives, roughly chopped

salt and pepper

Melt the butter with the oil in a saucepan, add the onion and garlic and cook for about 3 minutes until soft. Add the rice and stir until coated with the butter mixture. Add the wine and cook rapidly, stirring, until it has evaporated.

Add the hot stock, a ladleful at a time, and cook, stirring constantly, until each addition has been absorbed before adding the next. Continue until all the stock has been absorbed and the rice is creamy and cooked but still retains a little bite – this will take around 15 minutes.

Stir in the spinach and zucchinis and heat through for 3–5 minutes. Remove from the heat and stir in the cheese and herbs. Season to taste with salt and pepper and serve immediately.

Summer is the perfect time to get out into the garden. Gardening is a great way to enjoy the outdoors and will help you burn some calories, as a bonus.

fruit skewers with rosewater dressing

THE SCIENCE BIT

The combination of pineapple, strawberries and kiwis in these sweet and tangy skewers offers a real hit of vitamins A, C, K and E.

SERVES 4

Prep + cook time: 20 minutes
 + cooling

350 ml (12 fl oz) guava, apple or
 raspberry and guava juice
2 tablespoons rosewater
3 cardamom pods, lightly crushed
2 star anise
2 tablespoons soft light brown sugar
1 papaya, cut in half, deseeded and
 cut into chunks
2 kiwifruit, peeled and cut into
 chunks
1 small pineapple, peeled, cored and
 cut into chunks
250 g (8 oz) strawberries, hulled and
 halved if large

Pour the fruit juice and rosewater into a small saucepan, add the cardamom, star anise and sugar and place over a low heat. Stir to dissolve the sugar, then simmer gently for 5–6 minutes until fragrant. Pour into a large, shallow bowl and set aside to cool.

Meanwhile, thread the chunks of papaya, kiwifruit and pineapple alternately on to 8 skewers and arrange 2 skewers per person on serving plates.

Strain the dressing into a jug to remove the spices and drizzle over the fruit skewers before serving.

Made by steeping rose petals in water, rosewater is popular as a flavoring in Middle Eastern, Indian and Chinese cuisines. Add it to cakes and milky puddings, try a little sprinkled on a rice or couscous salad or add a few drops to a glass of sparkling water for a deliciously refreshing drink.

pumpkin soup with olive salsa

THE SCIENCE BIT
Go-to food when the temperatures plummet, warming soup on a dark and cold night provides comfort and a wide range of nutrients.

SERVES 6
Prep + cook time: 1 hour

4 tablespoons olive oil
1 large onion, chopped
2 garlic cloves, crushed
1 tablespoon chopped sage
1 kg (2 lb) peeled, deseeded
    pumpkin, cubed
400 g (13 oz) can cannellini or
    haricot beans, rinsed and drained
1 litre (1¾ pints) vegetable stock
    (see page 9 for homemade)
salt and pepper

olive salsa
100 g (3½ oz) pitted black olives
3 tablespoons extra-virgin olive oil
grated rind of 1 lemon
2 tablespoons chopped parsley

Heat the oil in a saucepan, add the onion, garlic and sage and cook over a low heat, stirring frequently, for 5 minutes. Add the pumpkin and beans and stir well, then add the stock and a little salt and pepper.

Bring to the boil, then reduce the heat, cover and simmer gently for 30 minutes until the pumpkin is tender. Blend until smooth and adjust seasoning.

Meanwhile, make the salsa. Chop the olives and mix with the oil, lemon rind, parsley and salt and pepper in a bowl.

Ladle the soup into bowls and top with spoonfuls of the salsa.

Like sweet potatoes and carrots and other bright orange veg, pumpkins boast the antioxidant beta-carotene, which may play a role in cancer prevention.

mushroom, cauliflower & chickpea stew

THE SCIENCE BIT

Betaglucans contained in mushrooms appear to boost immunity and help resistance against allergies.

SERVES 4

Prep + cook time: 30 minutes

2 tablespoons sunflower oil

8 scallions, cut into 5 cm
  (2 inch) lengths

2 teaspoons grated garlic

2 teaspoons ground ginger

2 tablespoons hot curry powder

200 g (7 oz) baby button mushrooms

300 g (10 oz) cauliflower florets

2 red peppers, cored, deseeded and
  cut into chunks

400 g (13 oz) can chopped
  tomatoes

220 g (7½ oz) can chickpeas, rinsed
  and drained

3–4 tablespoons natural yogurt

salt and pepper

large handful of chopped mint
  leaves, to garnish

warm naan bread or steamed rice,
  to serve

Heat the oil in a large frying pan, add the scallions and fry over a medium heat for 1–2 minutes. Add the garlic, ground ginger and curry powder and fry, stirring, for 20–30 seconds until fragrant, then stir in the mushrooms, cauliflower and red peppers and fry for a further 2–3 minutes.

Stir in the tomatoes and bring to the boil. Cover, then reduce the heat to medium and simmer, uncovered, for 10–15 minutes, stirring occasionally. Add the chickpeas, season with salt and pepper and bring back to the boil.

Spoon into bowls, drizzle with the yogurt and scatter with chopped mint. Serve with warm naan bread or steamed rice.

Part of the cruciferous vegetable family, along with broccoli, kale and cabbage, cauliflower has plenty of health benefits, including large amounts of vitamin A, thiamine, riboflavin, niacin, calcium and iron.

lentil & parsnip cottage pie

THE SCIENCE BIT

Try to avoid "treating" yourself
to sugary and fat-laden food
as it gets colder. Instead opt for
slow-release carbs to keep
your mood in balance.

SERVES 6

Prep + cook time: 1 hour

1 tablespoon sunflower oil
1 large onion, chopped
2 celery sticks, finely sliced
4 carrots, chopped
250 g (8 oz) chestnut mushrooms,
   chopped
2 × 400 g (13 oz) cans green lentils
   in water, rinsed and drained
400 g (13 oz) can chopped tomatoes
1 tablespoon tomato purée
300 ml (½ pint) vegetable stock
   (see page 9 for homemade)
2 teaspoons dried mixed herbs
500 g (1 lb) parsnips, peeled and
   chopped
500 g (1 lb) floury potatoes, peeled
   and chopped
2 tablespoons milk
25 g (1 oz) butter
50 g (2 oz) Cheddar cheese, grated
salt and pepper

Heat the oil in a large saucepan, add the onion, celery and carrots and cook for 3–4 minutes until softened. Increase the heat, stir in the mushrooms and cook for a further 3 minutes, stirring occasionally.

Add the lentils, tomatoes, tomato purée, stock and mixed herbs. Bring to the boil, then reduce the heat and simmer, uncovered, for 15 minutes. Season to taste with salt and pepper. Transfer to a 2 litre (3½ pint) ovenproof dish.

Meanwhile, cook the parsnips and potatoes in a large saucepan of lightly salted boiling water for 20 minutes or until tender.

Drain the root vegetables and return to the pan. Mash with the milk and butter, then season to taste with salt and pepper.

Spoon the parsnip mash over the lentil mixture and scatter over the cheese. Bake in a preheated oven, 190°C (375°F) for 20 minutes until golden and bubbling.

chestnut mushroom & spinach pilau

THE SCIENCE BIT

In addition to providing rich flavor, fragrant cardamom also offers a number of nutritional benefits, including essential minerals and fiber.

SERVES 4

Prep + cook time: 40 minutes

2 tablespoons vegetable oil
1 onion, finely chopped
2 garlic cloves, finely chopped
200 g (7 oz) chestnut mushrooms, diced
3 cardamom pods, lightly crushed
¼ teaspoon ground cloves
½ teaspoon ground cinnamon
150 g (5 oz) basmati rice
500 ml (17 fl oz) hot vegetable stock (see page 9 for homemade)
125 g (4 oz) frozen peas, defrosted
125 g (4 oz) spinach leaves, roughly chopped
salt and pepper
fried onions, to garnish (optional)

Heat the oil in a large, deep-sided frying pan and cook the onion and garlic for 4–5 minutes over a medium-high heat, stirring occasionally, until beginning to color.

Add the mushrooms, cook for 2 minutes, then add the spices and rice and stir for 1 minute.

Pour in the stock, season generously and cover with a tight-fitting lid. Simmer very gently for about 15 minutes, until the rice grains are almost tender.

Remove from the heat and fold in the peas and spinach. Replace the lid and set aside for 4–5 minutes, until the liquid has been absorbed and the rice is tender and light. Serve garnished with fried onions, if liked.

The best way to store mushrooms is in a paper bag in the fridge. Don't store them in a plastic bag, because they will sweat and quickly spoil.

vegetable broth with pearl barley

THE SCIENCE BIT

Ideal for adding body and nutrition to vegetarian soups and stews, pearl barley is barley that has been processed to remove its hull and bran.

SERVES 4

Prep + cook time: 1 hour 45 minutes

100 g (3½ oz) pearl barley
2 tablespoons extra-virgin rapeseed oil
1 large onion, finely chopped
2 leeks, trimmed, cleaned and finely chopped
1 celery stick, finely chopped
750 g (1½ lb) mixed root vegetables such as parsnips, swede, turnips, carrots and potatoes, evenly diced
1.2 litres (2 pints) vegetable stock (see page 9 for homemade)
1 bouquet garni
salt and pepper
herby bread, to serve (optional)

Bring a large saucepan of water to the boil and pour in the pearl barley. Cook at a gentle simmer for 1 hour. Drain well.

Meanwhile, heat the oil in a large, heavy-based saucepan over a medium-low heat, add the onion, leeks and celery and fry gently for 8–10 minutes or until softened but not colored. Add the root vegetables and cook for a further 5 minutes, stirring regularly.

Pour in the stock, add the bouquet garni and bring to the boil. Stir in the pearl barley, then reduce the heat and simmer for 25–30 minutes or until the vegetables and pearl barley are tender. Remove the bouquet garni and season to taste with salt and pepper. Ladle into bowls and serve with herby bread, if liked.

French for "garnished bouquet", a bouquet garni is a bundle of aromatic herbs, usually tied together or in muslin bag, which can be added to casseroles, sauces and soups.

winter fruits with orange ricotta

THE SCIENCE BIT

This delicious combination of fresh and dried fruit, topped with creamy ricotta, is jam-packed with vitamin C to boost immunity.

SERVES 4

Prep + cook time: 20 minutes
 + standing

100 g (3½ oz) ready-to-eat dried
 apricots, roughly chopped
100 g (3½ oz) dried figs, chopped
100 g (3½ oz) prunes, pitted
2 tablespoons raisins
2 tablespoons dried cherries
2 plums, halved and pitted
1 pear, peeled cut into wedges
3 tablespoons orange juice
grated rind of 2 oranges
3 tablespoons honey
100 ml (3½ fl oz) boiling water
250 g (8 oz) ricotta cheese
100 g (3½ oz) natural yogurt

Stir together all the fruit, 2 tablespoons of the orange juice, the grated rind of 1 orange and 2 tablespoons of the honey in a saucepan. Pour in the measurement water and bring to a gentle simmer, then cook for 6–7 minutes, stirring occasionally. Leave to stand for 8–10 minutes.

Meanwhile, beat together the remaining orange juice, orange rind and honey with the ricotta and yogurt in a large bowl.

Spoon the winter fruits into 4 bowls and serve with the orange ricotta.

It's important to take care of your health throughout the year, but in winter it becomes even more essential so aim to eat well, get enough sleep and stay active.

root vegetable & bean crumble

THE SCIENCE BIT

With a low glycaemic index, beans contain an ideal blend of complex carbohydrates and protein so are digested slowly, which helps keep blood glucose stable.

SERVES 4–6

Prep + cook time: 1 hour 15 minutes

1 tablespoon olive oil
2 carrots, sliced
2 parsnips, peeled and chopped
2 leeks, trimmed, cleaned and sliced
300 ml (½ pint) red wine
400 g (13 oz) can chopped tomatoes
300 ml (½ pint) vegetable stock
  (see page 9 for homemade)
400 g (13 oz) can butter beans,
  rinsed and drained
1 tablespoon chopped rosemary
salt and pepper

crumble topping
100 g (3½ oz) sliced wholemeal
  bread, roughly torn into pieces
50 g (2 oz) walnuts, roughly chopped
2 tablespoons chopped flat leaf
  parsley
100 g (3½ oz) Wensleydale or
  Lancashire cheese, crumbled

Heat the oil in a large saucepan, add the carrots, parsnips and leeks and cook over a medium heat for 4–5 minutes until slightly softened.

Stir the wine into the pan and cook until reduced by half, then stir in the tomatoes, stock, butter beans and rosemary. Season well with salt and pepper, then cover and simmer for 15 minutes, stirring occasionally. Transfer to a 2 litre (3½ pint) ovenproof dish.

Meanwhile, make the crumble topping. Place the bread, walnuts, parsley and 75 g (3 oz) of the cheese in a food processor and legume until the mixture resembles breadcrumbs.

Spoon the topping over the vegetable mixture and scatter over the remaining cheese. Bake in a preheated oven, 180°C (350°F) for 25–30 minutes until golden and crisp. Remove from oven and serve immediately.

mushroom stroganoff

THE SCIENCE BIT

Mushrooms are a valuable part of the diet, being a good source of B vitamins and essential minerals potassium, selenium, copper and phosphorus.

SERVES 4
Prep + cook time: 20 minutes

1 tablespoon butter
2 tablespoons olive oil
1 onion, thinly sliced
4 garlic cloves, finely chopped
500 g (1 lb) chestnut mushrooms, sliced
2 tablespoons wholegrain mustard
250 ml (8 fl oz) crème fraîche
salt and pepper
3 tablespoons chopped parsley, to garnish

Melt the butter with the oil in a large frying pan, add the onion and garlic and cook until soft and starting to brown.

Add the mushrooms to the pan and cook until soft and starting to brown. Stir in the mustard and crème fraîche and just heat through. Season to taste with salt and pepper, then serve immediately, garnished with the chopped parsley.

It can be appealing to hibernate during winter, but you will notice the difference if you get outside for some exercise. It keeps you in shape and stimulates serotonin for an instant mood boost.

index

ACKNOWLEDGEMENTS

123RF/ABImages 114 right. Inna Astakhova 45 right, 56 left, 64 left, 65 left, 86 left and right, 92 left, 104 left, 124 right, 142 left, 145 left, 164 left. Aleksandr Belugin 15 right, 64 right, 154 right. Pichest Boonpanchua 45 left, 29 right, 34 left, 136 right. Sylwia Brataniec 19 left, 104 right. cloud7days 16 left, 50 left, 114 left, 148 right. Kitz Corner 130–131. Olena Danileiko 78–79. Yuliia Davydenko 101 left, 108 left, 140 left. digifuture 126 left. Hataigan Doungbal 52 left. Peter Hermes Furian 57 right, 93 left, 166 left, 173 left. Yuliya Gontar 80–81. Andrii Gorulko 30 left and right, 99 left, 111 right, 125 left, 137 right, 142 right, 164 right. Andrii Hrytsenko 16 right, 22 left, 51 right, 156 right. Komain Intaramhaeng 15 left, 40 right, 90 left, 110 right, 133 right. Iquaca 42 left, 23 left, 61 right, 115 right, 148 left. Jirkaejc 103 left, 119 right. Sataporin Jiwjalaen 102 right. karandaev 4–5, 149 left. Sergey Kolesnikov 61 left. Sommai Larkjit 24 left, 29 left, 34 right, 42 right, 46 left, 55 left, 71 left, 84, 90 right, 99 right, 152 right, 153 left, 159, 163 right. Robyn Mackenzie 7, 156 left. Markus Mainka 6. Andrey Maslakov 1. Riccardo Motti 43 right. movingmoment 2–3. Maksym Narodenko 40 left. Leonid Nyshko 156 left. Nipaporn Panyacharoen 103 right. Baiba Opule 36 right, 33 left, 73 right, 74 left, 83 left, 95 left, 107 right, 120 left, 149 right, 165 left. Dmytro Pauk 146 left. Penchan Pumila 102 left, 137 left. Roberts Resnais 19 right. Volodymyr Shevchuk 134 right. Danny Smythe 22 right. spafra 58 right, 77 right, 85 right, 163 right. tan4ikk 89 right, 98 right, 113 right, 126 right, 146 right. Oleksii Terpugov 18 left, 172 right. Nuttapong Ternmongkol 120 right, 125 right. tobi 52 right, 151 right. Marek Uliasz 39 left, 43 left. victor69 128–129. Victoria Shibut 10–11, 12–13. Edward Westmacott 57 left, 133 left, 140 right. wimi 124 left. yurakp 74 right.

Dreamstime.com/Andreykuzmin 85 left. Cretolamna 169 right. Adrian Ciurea 39 right, 101 right. Sergey Galushko 56 right, 95 right, 173 right. Goodween123 50 right. Petr Goskov 21 left, 49 right, 58 right, 62 left. Hamsterman 136 left, 153 right, 169 right. HandmadePictures 26 left. Jirkaejc 70 right, 107 left, 165 right. Katerina Kovaleva 154 left. Viktor Kunz 33 right, 70 left, 115 left, 116 right, 134 left. 172 left. Alexander Levchenko 139 right, 170 left. Leo Lintag 139 left. Olga Lupol 111 left. Marie Maerz 55 right, 92 right, 151 left. Marcomayer 27 left, 76 right. Sergeii Moskaliuk 96 right. Ovydyborets 35 left. Pjirawat 65 right, 119 left. Radub85 27 right, 76 left, 170 right. Valentina Razumova 18 right, 24 right, 67 right. Renzzo 98 left, 116 left, 156 right, 166 right. Yordan Rusev 35 right. Sierpniowka 169 left. Danny Smythe 46 right. Sommai 21 right, 26 right, 49 left, 71 right, 74 left, 83 right, 108 right, 145 right. Pavel Sytsko 36 left, 141 right. Jiri Vaclavek 93 right, 110 left, 141 left. yuralp 88 left, 96 left, 113 left, 123 left.

Octopus Publishing Group/Stephen Conroy 121. Will Heap 32, 47, 48, 53, 54, 94, 106, 117, 135, 150, 167. David Munns 147. Lis Parsons 59, 75, 82, 87, 91, 97, 100, 105, 109, 112, 118, 132, 161, 170. Bill Reavell 127, 155, 158. Craig Robertson 25. William Shaw 17, 20, 28, 31, 37, 38, 44, 60, 63, 66, 72, 88, 138, 122, 144, 169. Ian Wallace 14, 41, 69, 163.